John Ruskin

The Queen of the Air

A Study of the Greek Myths of Cloud and Storm

John Ruskin

The Queen of the Air
A Study of the Greek Myths of Cloud and Storm

ISBN/EAN: 9783337340988

Printed in Europe, USA, Canada, Australia, Japan

Cover: Foto ©Lupo / pixelio.de

More available books at **www.hansebooks.com**

THE
QUEEN OF THE AIR:

BEING

A STUDY OF THE GREEK MYTHS

OF

CLOUD AND STORM.

BY

JOHN RUSKIN, LL.D.

NEW YORK:

JOHN WILEY & SON, PUBLISHERS,

15 ASTOR PLACE.

1871.

PREFACE.

My days and strength have lately been much broken; and I never more felt the insufficiency of both than in preparing for the press the following desultory memoranda on a most noble subject. But I leave them now as they stand, for no time nor labour would be enough to complete them to my contentment; and I believe that they contain suggestions which may be followed with safety, by persons who are beginning to take interest in the aspects of mythology, which only recent investigation has removed from the region of conjecture into that of rational inquiry. I have some advantage, also, from my field work, in the interpretation of myths relating to natural phenomena; and I have had always near me, since we were at college together, a sure, and unweariedly kind, guide, in my friend Charles Newton, to whom we owe the finding of more treasure in mines of marble, than, were it rightly estimated, all California could buy. I must not, however, permit the chance of his name being in any wise associated with my errors. Much of my work has been done obstinately in my own way; and he is never responsible for me, though he has often kept me right, or at least enabled me to advance in a right direction. Absolutely right no one can be in such matters; nor does a day pass without convincing every honest student of antiquity of some partial error, and showing him better how to think, and where to look. But I knew that there was no hope of my being able to enter with advantage on the fields of history opened by the splendid investigation of recent philologists; though I could qualify myself, by attention and sympathy, to understand here and there, a verse of Homer's or Hesiod's, as the simple people did for whom they sang.

Even while I correct these sheets for press, a lecture by Professor Tyndall has been put into my hands, which I ought to have heard last 16th of January, but was hindered by mischance; and which, I now find, completes, in two important particulars, the evidence of an instinctive truth in ancient symbolism; showing, first, that the Greek conception of an ætherial element pervading space is justified by the closest reasoning of modern physicists; and, secondly, that the blue of the sky, hitherto thought to be caused by watery vapour, is, indeed, reflected from the divided air itself; so that the bright blue of the eyes of Athena, and the deep blue of her ægis, prove to be accurate mythic expressions of natural phenomena which it is an uttermost triumph of recent science to have revealed.

Indeed, it would be difficult to imagine triumph more complete. To form, "within an experimental tube, a bit of more perfect sky than the sky itself!" here is magic of the finest sort! singularly reversed from that of old time, which only asserted its competency to enclose in bottles elemental forces that were—not of the sky.

Let me, in thanking Professor Tyndall for the true wonder of this piece of work, ask his pardon, and that of all masters in physical science, for any words of mine, either in the following pages or elsewhere, that may ever seem to fail in the respect due to their great powers of thought, or in the admiration due to the far scope of their discovery. But I will be judged by themselves, if I have not bitter reason to ask them to teach us more than yet they have taught.

This first day of May, 1869, I am writing where my work was begun thirty-five years ago,—within sight of the snows of the higher Alps. In that half of the permitted life of man, I have seen strange evil brought upon every scene that I best loved, or tried to make beloved by others. The light which once flushed those pale summits with its rose at dawn, and purple at sunset, is now umbered and faint; the air which once inlaid the clefts of all their golden crags with azure, is now defiled with languid coils of smoke, belched from worse than volcanic fires; their very glacier waves are ebbing, and their snows fading, as if Hell had breathed on them; the waters that once sank at their feet into crystalline rest, are now dimmed and foul, from deep to deep, and shore to shore. These are no careless words—they are accurately—horribly—true. I know what the Swiss lakes were; no pool of Alpine fountain at its source was clearer. This morning, on the Lake of Geneva, at half a mile from the beach, I could scarcely see my oar-blade a fathom deep.

The light, the air, the waters, all defiled! How of the earth itself? Take this one fact for type of honour done by the modern Swiss to the earth of his native land. There used to be a little rock at the end of the avenue by the port of Neuchâtel; there, the last marble of the foot of Jura, sloping to the blue water, and (at this time of year) covered with bright pink tufts of Saponaria. I went, three days since, to gather a blossom at the place. The goodly native rock and its flowers were covered with the dust and refuse of the town; but, in the middle of the avenue, was a newly-constructed artificial rockery, with a fountain twisted through a spinning spout, and an inscription on one of its loose-tumbled stones,—

"Aux Botanistes,
Le club Jurassique."

Ah, masters of modern science, give me back my Athena out of your vials, and seal, if it may be, once more, Asmodeus therein. You have divided the elements, and united them; enslaved them upon the earth, and discerned them in the stars. Teach us, now, but this of them, which is all that man need know,—that the Air is given to him for his life; and the Rain to his thirst, and for his baptism; and the Fire for warmth; and the Sun for sight; and the Earth for his meat—and his Rest.

VEVAY, May 1, 1869.

THE QUEEN OF THE AIR.

I.

ATHENA CHALINITIS.*

(*Athena in the Heavens.*)

Lecture on the Greek Myths of Storm, given (partly,) in University College, London, March 9th, 1869.

1. I WILL not ask your pardon for endeavouring to interest you in the subject of Greek Mythology; but I must ask your permission to approach it in a temper differing from that in which it is frequently treated. We cannot justly interpret the religion of any people, unless we are prepared to admit that we ourselves, as well as they, are liable to error in matters of faith ; and that the convictions of others, however singular, may in some points have been well founded, while our own, however reasonable, may in some particulars be mistaken. You must forgive me, therefore, for not always distinctively calling the creeds of the past "superstition," and the creeds of the present day " religion ; " as well as for assuming that a faith now confessed may sometimes be superficial, and that a faith long forgotten may once have been sincere. It is the task of the

---

* "Athena the Restrainer." The name is given to her as having helped Bellerophon to bridle Pegasus, the flying cloud.

Divine to condemn the errors of antiquity, and of the Philologist to account for them: I will only pray you to read, with patience, and human sympathy, the thoughts of men who lived without blame in a darkness they could not dispel; and to remember that, whatever charge of folly may justly attach to the saying,—" There is no God," the folly is prouder, deeper, and less pardonable, in saying, " There is no God but for me."

2. A Myth, in its simplest definition, is a story with a meaning attached to it, other than it seems to have at first; and the fact that it has such a meaning is generally marked by some of its circumstances being extraordinary, or, in the common use of the word, unnatural. Thus, if I tell you that Hercules killed a water-serpent in the lake of Lerna, and if I mean, and you understand, nothing more than that fact, the story, whether true or false, is not a myth. But if by telling you this, I mean that Hercules purified the stagnation of many streams from deadly miasmata, my story, however simple, is a true myth; only, as, if I left it in that simplicity, you would probably look for nothing beyond, it will be wise in me to surprise your attention by adding some singular circumstance; for instance, that the water-snake had several heads, which revived as fast as they were killed, and which poisoned even the foot that trode upon them as they slept. And in proportion to the fulness of intended meaning I shall probably multiply and refine upon these improbabilities; as, suppose, if, instead of desiring only to tell you that Hercules purified a marsh, I wished you to understand that he contended with the

venom and vapour of envy and evil ambition, whether in other men's souls or in his own, and choked *that* malaria only by supreme toil,—I might tell you that this serpent was formed by the Goddess whose pride was in the trial of Hercules; and that its place of abode was by a palm-tree; and that for every head of it that was cut off, two rose up with renewed life; and that the hero found at last he could not kill the creature at all by cutting its heads off or crushing them; but only by burning them down; and that the midmost of them could not be killed even that way, but had to be buried alive. Only in proportion as I mean more, I shall certainly appear more absurd in my statement; and at last, when I get unendurably significant, all practical persons will agree that I was talking mere nonsense from the beginning, and never meant anything at all.

3. It is just possible, however, also, that the story-teller may all along have meant nothing but what he said; and that, incredible as the events may appear, he himself literally believed—and expected you also to believe—all this about Hercules, without any latent moral or history whatever. And it is very necessary, in reading traditions of this kind, to determine, first of all, whether you are listening to a simple person, who is relating what, at all events, he believes to be true (and may, therefore, possibly have been so to some extent), or to a reserved philosopher, who is veiling a theory of the universe under the grotesque of a fairy tale. It is, in general, more likely that the first supposition should be the right one:—simple and credu-

lous persons are, perhaps fortunately, more common than philosophers: and it is of the highest importance that you should take their innocent testimony as it was meant, and not efface, under the graceful explanation which your cultivated ingenuity may suggest, either the evidence their story may contain (such as it is worth) of an extraordinary event having really taken place, or the unquestionable light which it will cast upon the character of the person by whom it was frankly believed. And to deal with Greek religion honestly, you must at once understand that this literal belief was, in the mind of the general people, as deeply rooted as ours in the legends of our own sacred book; and that a basis of unmiraculous event was as little suspected, and an explanatory symbolism as rarely traced, by them, as by us.

You must, therefore, observe that I deeply degrade the position which such a myth as that just referred to occupied in the Greek mind, by comparing it (for fear of offending you) to our story of St. George and the Dragon. Still, the analogy is perfect in minor respects; and though it fails to give you any notion of the vitally religious earnestness of the Greek faith, it will exactly illustrate the manner in which faith laid hold of its objects.

4. This story of Hercules and the Hydra, then, was to the general Greek mind, in its best days, a tale about a real hero and a real monster. Not one in a thousand knew anything of the way in which the story had arisen, any more than the English peasant generally is aware of the plebeian origin of St. George; or supposes that there were

once alive in the world, with sharp teeth and claws, real, and very ugly, flying dragons. On the other hand, few persons traced any moral or symbolical meaning in the story, and the average Greek was as far from imagining any interpretation like that I have just given you, as an average Englishman is from seeing in St. George the Red Cross Knight of Spenser, or in the Dragon the Spirit of Infidelity. But, for all that, there was a certain undercurrent of consciousness in all minds, that the figures meant more than they at first showed; and, according to each man's own faculties of sentiment, he judged and read them; just as a Knight of the Garter reads more in the jewel on his collar than the George and Dragon of a public-house expresses to the host or to his customers. Thus, to the mean person the myth always meant little; to the noble person, much: and the greater their familiarity with it, the more contemptible it became to the one, and the more sacred to the other: until vulgar commentators explained it entirely away, while Virgil made it the crowning glory of his choral hymn to Hercules:

> " Around thee, powerless to infect thy soul,
> Rose, in his crested crowd, the Lerna worm."

> " Non te rationis egentem
> Lernæus turbâ capitum circumstetit anguis."

And although, in any special toil of the hero's life, the moral interpretation was rarely with definiteness attached to its event, yet in the whole course of the life, not only a symbolical meaning, but the warrant for the existence of a real spiritual power, was apprehended of all men. Hercules was no dead hero, to be remembered only as a victor over monsters of the past—harmless now, as slain. He was the perpetual type and mirror of heroism, and its present and living aid against every ravenous form of human trial and pain.

5. But, if we seek to know more than this, and to ascertain the manner in which the story first crystallized into its shape, we shall find ourselves led back generally to one or other of two sources—either to actual historical events, represented by the fancy under figures personifying them; or else to natural phenomena similarly endowed with life by the imaginative power, usually more or less under the influence of terror. The historical myths we must leave the masters of history to follow; they, and the events they record, being yet involved in great, though attractive and penetrable, mystery. But the stars, and hills, and storms are with us now, as they were with others of old; and it only needs that we look at them with the earnestness of those childish eyes to understand the first words spoken of them by the children of men. And then, in all the most beautiful and enduring myths, we shall find, not only a literal story of a real person,—not only a parallel imagery of moral principle,—but an underlying worship of natural phenomena, out of which both have sprung, and in which both for ever remain rooted. Thus, from the real sun, rising and setting;—from the real atmosphere, calm in its dominion of unfading blue, and fierce in its descent of tempest,—the Greek forms first the

idea of two entirely personal and corporeal gods, whose limbs are clothed in divine flesh, and whose brows are crowned with divine beauty; yet so real that the quiver rattles at their shoulder, and the chariot bends beneath their weight. And, on the other hand, collaterally with these corporeal images, and never for one instant separated from them, he conceives also two omnipresent spiritual influences, of which one illuminates, as the sun, with a constant fire, whatever in humanity is skilful and wise; and the other, like the living air, breathes the calm of heavenly fortitude, and strength of righteous anger, into every human breast that is pure and brave.

6. Now, therefore, in nearly every myth of importance, and certainly in every one of those of which I shall speak to-night, you have to discern these three structural parts— the root and the two branches :—the root, in physical existence, sun, or sky, or cloud, or sea; then the personal incarnation of that; becoming a trusted and companionable deity, with whom you may walk hand in hand, as a child with its brother or its sister; and, lastly, the moral significance of the image, which is in all the great myths eternally and beneficently true.

7. The great myths; that is to say, myths made by great people. For the first plain fact about myth-making is one which has been most strangely lost sight of,—that you cannot make a myth unless you have something to make it of. You cannot tell a secret which you don't know. If the myth is about the sky, it must have been made by somebody who had looked at the sky. If the myth is about

justice and fortitude, it must have been made by some one who knew what it was to be just or patient. According to the quantity of understanding in the person will be the quantity of significance in his fable; and the myth of a simple and ignorant race must necessarily mean little, because a simple and ignorant race have little to mean. So the great question in reading a story is always, not what wild hunter dreamed, or what childish race first dreaded it; but what wise man first perfectly told, and what strong people first perfectly lived by it. And the real meaning of any myth is that which it has at the noblest age of the nation among whom it is current. The farther back you pierce, the less significance you will find, until you come to the first narrow thought, which, indeed, contains the germ of the accomplished tradition; but only as the seed contains the flower. As the intelligence and passion of the race develop, they cling to and nourish their beloved and sacred legend; leaf by leaf it expands under the touch of more pure affections, and more delicate imagination, until at last the perfect fable burgeons out into symmetry of milky stem, and honied bell.

8. But through whatever changes it may pass, remember that our right reading of it is wholly dependent on the materials we have in our own minds for an intelligent answering sympathy. If it first arose among a people who dwelt under stainless skies, and measured their journeys by ascending and declining stars, we certainly cannot read their story, if we have never seen anything above us in the day, but smoke; nor anything round us in the night but

candles. If the tale goes on to change clouds or planets into living creatures,—to invest them with fair forms—and inflame them with mighty passions, we can only understand the story of the human-hearted things, in so far as we ourselves take pleasure in the perfectness of visible form, or can sympathize, by an effort of imagination, with the strange people who had other loves than that of wealth, and other interests than those of commerce. And, lastly, if the myth complete itself to the fulfilled thoughts of the nation, by attributing to the gods, whom they have carved out of their fantasy, continual presence with their own souls; and their every effort for good is finally guided by the sense of the companionship, the praise, and the pure will of Immortals, we shall be able to follow them into this last circle of their faith only in the degree in which the better parts of our own beings have been also stirred by the aspects of nature, or strengthened by her laws. It may be easy to prove that the ascent of Apollo in his chariot signifies nothing but the rising of the sun. But what does the sunrise itself signify to us? If only languid return to frivolous amusement, or fruitless labour, it will, indeed, not be easy for us to conceive the power, over a Greek, of the name of Apollo. But if, for us also, as for the Greek, the sunrise means daily restoration to the sense of passionate gladness and of perfect life—if it means the thrilling of new strength through every nerve,—the shedding over us of a better peace than the peace of night, in the power of the dawn,—and the purging of evil vision and fear by the baptism of its dew;—if the sun itself is an influence, to us also, of spiritual good—and becomes thus in reality, not in imagination, to us also, a spiritual power,—we may then soon over-pass the narrow limit of conception which kept that power impersonal, and rise with the Greek to the thought of an angel who rejoiced as a strong man to run his course, whose voice, calling to life and to labour, rang round the earth, and whose going forth was to the ends of heaven.

9. The time, then, at which I shall take up for you, as well as I can decipher it, the tradition of the Gods of Greece, shall be near the beginning of its central and formed faith,—about 500 B.C.,—a faith of which the character is perfectly represented by Pindar and Æschylus, who are both of them outspokenly religious, and entirely sincere men; while we may always look back to find the less developed thought of the preceding epoch given by Homer, in a more occult, subtle, half-instinctive and involuntary way.

10. Now, at that culminating period of the Greek religion we find, under one governing Lord of all things, four subordinate elemental forces, and four spiritual powers living in them, and commanding them. The elements are of course the well-known four of the ancient world—the earth, the waters, the fire, and the air; and the living powers of them are Demeter, the Latin Ceres; Poseidon, the Latin Neptune; Apollo, who has retained always his Greek name; and Athena, the Latin Minerva. Each of these are descended from, or changed from, more ancient, and therefore more mystic deities of

the earth and heaven, and of a finer element of æther supposed to be beyond the heavens;* but at this time we find the four quite definite, both in their kingdoms and in their personalities. They are the rulers of the earth that we tread upon, and the air that we breathe ; and are with us as closely, in their vivid humanity, as the dust that they animate, and the winds that they bridle. I shall briefly define for you the range of their separate dominions, and then follow, as far as we have time, the most interesting of the legends which relate to the queen of the air.

11. The rule of the first spirit, Demeter, the earth mother, is over the earth, first, as the origin of all life—the dust from whence we were taken : secondly, as the receiver of all things back at last into silence—"Dust thou art, and unto dust shalt thou return." And, therefore, as the most tender image of this appearing and fading life, in the birth and fall of flowers, her daughter Proserpine plays in the fields of Sicily, and thence is torn away into darkness, and becomes the Queen of Fate—not merely of death, but of the gloom which closes over and ends, not beauty only, but sin ; and chiefly of sins the sin against the life she gave: so that she is, in her highest power, Persephone, the avenger and purifier of blood,— "The voice of thy brother's blood cries to me *out of the ground*." Then, side by side with this queen of the earth, we find a demigod of agriculture by the plough—the lord of grain, or of the thing ground by the mill. And it is a

* And by modern science now also asserted, and with probability argued, to exist.

singular proof of the simplicity of Greek character at this noble time, that of all representations left to us of their deities by their art, few are so frequent, and none perhaps so beautiful, as the symbol of this spirit of agriculture.

12. Then the dominant spirit of the element of water is Neptune, but subordinate to him are myriads of other water spirits, of whom Nereus is the chief, with Palæmon, and Leucothea, the "white lady" of the sea; and Thetis, and nymphs innumerable, who, like her, could "suffer a sea change," while the river deities had each independent power, according to the preciousness of their streams to the cities fed by them,—the "fountain Arethuse, and thou, honored flood, smooth sliding Mincius, crowned with vocal reeds." And, spiritually, this king of the waters is lord of the strength and daily flow of human life—he gives it material force and victory; which is the meaning of the dedication of the hair, as the sign of the strength of life, to the river of the native land.

13. Demeter, then, over the earth, and its giving and receiving of life. Neptune over the waters, and the flow and force of life,—always among the Greeks typified by the horse, which was to them as a crested sea-wave, animated and bridled. Then the third element, fire, has set over it two powers: over earthly fire, the assistant of human labour, is set Hephæstus, lord of all labour in which is the flush and the sweat of the brow; and over heavenly fire, the source of day, is set Apollo, the spirit of all kindling, purifying, and illuminating intellectual wisdom;

each of these gods having also their subordinate or associated powers—servant, or sister, or companion muse.

14. Then, lastly, we come to the myth which is to be our subject of closer inquiry—the story of Athena and of the deities subordinate to her. This great goddess, the Neith of the Egyptians, the Athena or Athenaia of the Greeks, and, with broken power, half usurped by Mars, the Minerva of the Latins, is, physically, the queen of the air; having supreme power both over its blessing of calm, and wrath of storm; and, spiritually, she is the queen of the breath of man, first of the bodily breathing which is life to his blood, and strength to his arm in battle; and then of the mental breathing, or inspiration, which is his moral health and habitual wisdom; wisdom of conduct and of the heart, as opposed to the wisdom of imagination and the brain; moral, as distinct from intellectual; inspired, as distinct from illuminated.

15. By a singular, and fortunate, though I believe wholly accidental coincidence, the heart-virtue, of which she is the spirit, was separated by the ancients into four divisions, which have since obtained acceptance from all men as rightly discerned, and have received, as if from the quarters of the four winds of which Athena is the natural queen, the name of "Cardinal" virtues: namely, Prudence, (the right seeing, and foreseeing, of events through darkness); Justice, (the righteous bestowal of favour and of indignation); Fortitude, (patience under trial by pain); and Temperance, (patience under trial by pleasure). With respect to these four virtues, the attributes of

Athena are all distinct. In her prudence, or sight in darkness, she is "Glaukopis," "owl-eyed."* In her justice, which is the dominant virtue, she wears two robes, one of light and one of darkness; the robe of light, saffron colour, or the colour of the daybreak, falls to her feet, covering her wholly with favour and love,—the calm of the sky in blessing; it is embroidered along its edge with her victory over the giants, (the troublous powers of the earth,) and the likeness of it was woven yearly by the Athenian maidens and carried to the temple of their own Athena,—not to the Parthenon, that was the temple of all the world's Athena,—but this they carried to the temple of their own only one, who loved them, and stayed with them always. Then her robe of indignation is worn on her breast and left arm only, fringed with fatal serpents, and fastened with Gorgonian cold, turning men to stone; physically, the lightning and the hail of chastisement by storm. Then in her fortitude she wears the crested and unstooping helmet;† and lastly, in her temperance, she is the queen of maidenhood—stainless as the air of heaven.

16. But all these virtues mass themselves in the Greek mind into the two main ones—of Justice, or noble passion, and Fortitude, or noble patience; and of these, the

* There are many other meanings in the epithet; see, farther on, § 91, p. 105.

† I am compelled, for clearness' sake, to mark only one neaning at a time. Athena's helmet is sometimes a mask—sometimes a sign of anger—sometimes of the highest light of æther; but I cannot speak of all this at once.

chief powers of Athena, the Greeks had divinely written for them, and for all men after them, two mighty songs,— one, of the Menis,* mens, passion, or zeal, of Athena, breathed into a mortal whose name is "Ache of heart," and whose short life is only the incarnate brooding and burst of storm; and the other is of the foresight and fortitude of Athena, maintained by her in the heart of a mortal whose name is given to him from a longer grief, Odysseus, the full of sorrow, the much-enduring, and the long-suffering. .

17. The minor expressions by the Greeks in word, in symbol, and in religious service, of this faith, are so many and so beautiful, that I hope some day to gather at least a few of them into a separate body of evidence respecting the power of Athena, and its relations to the ethical conception of the Homeric poems, or, rather, to their ethical nature; for they are not conceived didactically, but are didactic in their essence, as all good art is. There is an increasing insensibility to this character, and even an open denial of it, among us, now, which is one of the most curious errors of modernism,—the peculiar and judicial blindness of an age which, having long practised art and poetry for the sake of pleasure only, has become incapable of reading their language when they were both didactic: and also, having been itself accustomed to a professedly didactic teaching, which yet, for private

* This first word of the Iliad, Menis, afterwards passes into the Latin Mens; is the root of the Latin name for Athena, "Minerva," and so of the English "mind."

interests, studiously avoids collision with every prevalent vice of its day, (and especially with avarice), has become equally dead to the intensely ethical conceptions of a race which habitually divided all men into two broad classes of worthy or worthless;—good, and good for nothing. And even the celebrated passage of Horace about the Iliad is now misread or disbelieved, as if it was impossible that the Iliad could be instructive because it is not like a sermon. Horace does not say that it is like a sermon, and would have been still less likely to say so, if he ever had had the advantage of hearing a sermon. "I have been reading that story of Troy again" (thus he writes to a noble youth of Rome whom he cared for), "quietly at Præneste, while you have been busy at Rome; and truly I think that what is base and what is noble, and what useful and useless, may be better learned from that, than from all Chrysippus' and Crantor's talk put together."* Which is profoundly true, not of the Iliad only, but of all other great art whatsoever; for all pieces of such art are didactic in the purest way, indirectly and occultly, so that, first, you shall only be bettered by them if you are already hard at work in bettering yourself; and when you *are* bettered by them, it shall be partly with a general acceptance of their influence, so constant and subtle that you shall be no more conscious of it than of the healthy digestion of food; and partly by a gift of unexpected truth, which you

---

* Note, once for all, that unless when there is question about some particular expression, I never translate literally, but give the real force of what is said, as I best can, freely.

shall only find by slow mining for it;—which is withheld on purpose, and close-locked, that you may not get it till you have forged the key of it in a furnace of your own heating. And this withholding of their meaning is continual, and confessed, in the great poets. Thus Pindar says of himself: "There is many an arrow in my quiver, full of speech to the wise, but, for the many, they need interpreters." And neither Pindar, nor Æschylus, nor Hesiod, nor Homer, nor any of the greater poets or teachers of any nation or time, ever spoke but with intentional reservation: nay, beyond this, there is often a meaning which they themselves cannot interpret,—which it may be for ages long after them to interpret,—in what they said, so far as it recorded true imaginative vision. For all the greatest myths have been seen, by the men who tell them, involuntarily and passively,—seen by them with as great distinctness (and in some respects, though not in all, under conditions as far beyond the control of their will) as a dream sent to any of us by night when we dream clearest; and it is this veracity of vision that could not be refused, and of moral that could not be foreseen, which in modern historical inquiry has been left wholly out of account: being indeed the thing which no merely historical investigator can understand, or even believe; for it belongs exclusively to the creative or artistic group of men, and can only be interpreted by those of their race, who themselves in some measure also see visions and dream dreams.

So that you may obtain a more truthful idea of the

nature of Greek religion and legend from the poems of Keats, and the nearly as beautiful, and, in general grasp of subject, far more powerful, recent work of Morris, than from frigid scholarship, however extensive. Not that the poet's impressions or renderings of things are wholly true, but their truth is vital, not formal. They are like sketches from the life by Reynolds or Gainsborough, which may be demonstrably inaccurate or imaginary in many traits, and indistinct in others, yet will be in the deepest sense like, and true; while the work of historical analysis is too often weak with loss, through the very labour of its miniature touches, or useless in clumsy and rapid veracity of externals, and complacent security of having done all that is required for the portrait, when it has measured the breadth of the forehead, and the length of the nose.

18. The first of requirements, then, for the right reading of myths, is the understanding of the nature of all true vision by noble persons; namely, that it is founded on constant laws common to all human nature; that it perceives, however darkly, things which are for all ages true;—that we can only understand it so far as we have some perception of the same truth;—and that its fulness is developed and manifested more and more by the reverberation of it from minds of the same mirror-temper, in succeeding ages. You will understand Homer better by seeing his reflection in Dante, as you may trace new forms and softer colours in a hill-side, redoubled by a lake.

I shall be able partly to show you, even to-night, how

much, in the Homeric vision of Athena, has been made clearer by the advance of time, being thus essentially and eternally true; but I must in the outset indicate the relation to that central thought of the imagery of the inferior deities of storm.

19. And first I will take the myth of Æolus, (the "sage Hippotades" of Milton,) as it is delivered pure by Homer from the early times.

Why do you suppose Milton calls him "sage?" One does not usually think of the winds as very thoughtful or deliberate powers. But hear Homer: "Then we came to the Æolian island, and there dwelt Æolus Hippotades, dear to the deathless gods: there he dwelt in a floating island, and round it was a wall of brass that could not be broken; and the smooth rock of it ran up sheer. To whom twelve children were born in the sacred chambers—six daughters and six strong sons; and they dwell for ever with their beloved father, and their mother strict in duty; and with them are laid up a thousand benefits; and the misty house around them rings with fluting all the day long." Now, you are to note first, in this description, the wall of brass and the sheer rock. You will find, throughout the fables of the tempest-group, that the brazen wall and precipice (occurring in another myth as the brazen tower of Danae) are always connected with the idea of the towering cloud lighted by the sun, here truly described as a floating island. Secondly, you hear that all treasures were laid up in them; therefore, you know this Æolus is lord of the beneficent winds ("he bringeth the wind out of his treasuries"); and presently afterwards Homer calls him the "steward" of the winds, the master of the storehouse of them. And this idea of gifts and preciousness in the winds of heaven is carried out in the well-known sequel of the fable:—Æolus gives them to Ulysses, all but one, bound in leathern bags, with a glittering cord of silver; and so like bags of treasure that the sailors think they are so, and open them to see. And when Ulysses is thus driven back to Æolus, and prays him again to help him, note the deliberate words of the King's refusal,— " Did I not," he says, " send thee on thy way heartily, that thou mightest reach thy country, thy home, and whatever is dear to thee? It is not lawful for me again to send forth favourably on his journey a man hated by the happy gods." This idea of the beneficence of Æolus remains to the latest times, though Virgil, by adopting the vulgar change of the cloud island into Lipari, has lost it a little; but even when it is finally explained away by Diodorus, Æolus is still a kind-hearted monarch, who lived on the coast of Sorrento, invented the use of sails, and established a system of storm signals.

20. Another beneficent storm-power, Boreas, occupies an important place in early legend, and a singularly principal one in art; and I wish I could read to you a passage of Plato about the legend of Boreas and Oreithyia,* and the breeze and shade of the Ilissus—notwithstanding its

---

* Translated by Max Müller in the opening of his essay on "Comparative Mythology." (*Chips from a German Workshop*, vol. ii.)

severe reflection upon persons who waste their time on mythological studies: but I must go on at once to the fable with which you are all generally familiar, that of the Harpies.

This is always connected with that of Boreas or the north wind, because the two sons of Boreas are enemies of the Harpies, and drive them away into frantic flight. The myth in its first literal form means only the battle between the fair north wind and the foul south one: the two Harpies, "Stormswift" and "Swiftfoot," are the sisters of the rainbow—that is to say, they are the broken drifts of the showery south wind, and the clear north wind drives them back; but they quickly take a deeper and more malignant significance. You know the short, violent, spiral gusts that lift the dust before coming rain : the Harpies get identified first with these, and then with more violent whirlwinds, and so they are called "Harpies," "the Snatchers," and are thought of as entirely destructive; their manner of destroying being twofold—by snatching away, and by defiling and polluting. This is a month in which you may really see a small Harpy at her work almost whenever you choose. The first time that there is threatening of rain after two or three days of fine weather, leave your window well open to the street, and some books or papers on the table ; and if you do not, in a little while, know what the Harpies mean ; and how they snatch, and how they defile, I'll give up my Greek myths.

21. That is the physical meaning. It is now easy to find the mental one. You must all have felt the

expression of ignoble anger in those fitful gusts of sudden storm. There is a sense of provocation and apparent bitterness of purpose in their thin and senseless fury, wholly different from the noble anger of the greater tempests. Also, they seem useless and unnatural, and the Greek thinks of them always as vile in malice, and opposed, therefore, to the sons of Boreas, who are kindly winds, that fill sails, and wave harvests,—full of bracing health and happy impulses. From this lower and merely malicious temper, the Harpies rise into a greater terror, always associated with their whirling motion, which is indeed indicative of the most destructive winds: and they are thus related to the nobler tempests, as Charybdis to the sea; they are devouring and desolating, merciless, making all things disappear that come in their grasp: and so, spiritually, they are the gusts of vexatious, fretful, lawless passion, vain and overshadowing, discontented and lamenting, meagre and insane,—spirits of wasted energy, and wandering disease, and unappeased famine, and unsatisfied hope. So you have, on the one side, the winds of prosperity and health, on the other, of ruin and sickness. Understand that, once, deeply—any who have ever known the weariness of vain desires; the pitiful, unconquerable, coiling and recoiling and self-involved returns of some sickening famine and thirst of heart:—and you will know what was in the sound of the Harpy Celæno's shriek from her rock; and why, in the seventh circle of the "Inferno," the Harpies make their nests in the warped branches of the trees that are the souls of suicides.

22. Now you must always be prepared to read Greek legends as you trace threads through figures on a silken damask: the same thread runs through the web, but it makes part of different figures. Joined with other colours you hardly recognize it, and in different lights, it is dark or light. Thus the Greek fables blend and cross curiously in different directions, till they knit themselves into an arabesque where sometimes you cannot tell black from purple, nor blue from emerald—they being all the truer for this, because the truths of emotion they represent are interwoven in the same way, but all the more difficult to read, and to explain in any order. Thus the Harpies, as they represent vain desire, are connected with the Sirens, who are the spirits of constant desire: so that it is difficult sometimes in early art to know which are meant, both being represented alike as birds with women's heads; only the Sirens are the great constant desires—the infinite sicknesses of heart—which, rightly placed, give life, and wrongly placed, waste it away; so that there are two groups of Sirens, one noble and saving, as the other is fatal. But there are no animating or saving Harpies; their nature is always vexing and full of weariness, and thus they are curiously connected with the whole group of legends about Tantalus.

23. We all know what it is to be tantalized; but we do not often think of asking what Tantalus was tantalized for—what he had done, to be for ever kept hungry in sight of food? Well; he had not been condemned to this merely for being a glutton. By Dante the same punishment is

assigned to simple gluttony, to purge it away:—but the sins of Tantalus were of a much wider and more mysterious kind. There are four great sins attributed to him—one, stealing the food of the Gods to give it to men; another, sacrificing his son to feed the Gods themselves, (it may remind you for a moment of what I was telling you of the earthly character of Demeter, that, while the other Gods all refuse, she, dreaming about her lost daughter, eats part of the shoulder of Pelops before she knows what she is doing); another sin is, telling the secrets of the Gods; and only the fourth—stealing the golden dog of Pandareos—is connected with gluttony. The special sense of this myth is marked by Pandareos receiving the happy privilege of never being troubled with indigestion; the dog, in general, however, mythically represents all utterly senseless and carnal desires; mainly that of gluttony; and in the mythic sense of Hades—that is to say, so far as it represents spiritual ruin in this life, and not a literal hell—the dog Cerberus is its gate-keeper—with this special marking of his character of sensual passion, that he fawns on all those who descend, but rages against all who would return, (the Virgilian "facilis descensus" being a later recognition of this mythic character of Hades:) the last labour of Hercules is the dragging him up to the light; and in some sort, he represents the voracity or devouring of Hades itself; and the mediæval representation of the mouth of hell perpetuates the same thought. Then, also, the power of evil passion is partly associated with the red and scorching light of Sirius, as opposed to the pure light of the sun:—he is the dog-star of ruin; and hence the continual Homeric dwelling upon him, and comparison of the flame of anger to his swarthy light; only, in his scorching, it is thirst, not hunger, over which he rules physically; so that the fable of Icarius, his first master, corresponds, among the Greeks, to the legend of the drunkenness of Noah.

The story of Actæon, the raging death of Hecuba, and the tradition of the white dog which ate part of Hercules' first sacrifice, and so gave name to the Cynosarges, are all various phases of the same thought—the Greek notion of the dog being throughout confused between its serviceable fidelity, its watchfulness, its foul voracity, shamelessness, and deadly madness, while, with the curious reversal or recoil of the meaning which attaches itself to nearly every great myth—and which we shall presently see notably exemplified in the relations of the serpent to Athena,—the dog becomes in philosophy a type of severity and abstinence.

24. It would carry us too far aside were I to tell you the story of Pandareos' dog—or rather, of Jupiter's dog, for Pandareos was its guardian only; all that bears on our present purpose is that the guardian of this golden dog had three daughters, one of whom was subject to the power of the Sirens, and is turned into the nightingale; and the other two were subject to the power of the Harpies, and this was what happened to them. They were very beautiful, and they were beloved by the gods in their youth, and all the great goddesses were anxious to bring them up

rightly. Of all types of young ladies' education, there is nothing so splendid as that of the younger daughters of Pandareos. They have literally the four greatest goddesses for their governesses. Athena teaches them domestic accomplishments; how to weave, and sew, and the like; Artemis teaches them to hold themselves up straight; Hera, how to behave proudly and oppressively to company; and Aphrodite—delightful governess—feeds them with cakes and honey all day long. All goes well, until just the time when they are going to be brought out; then there is a great dispute whom they are to marry, and in the midst of it they are carried off by the Harpies, given by them to be slaves to the Furies, and never seen more. But of course there is nothing in Greek myths; and one never heard of such things as vain desires, and empty hopes, and clouded passions, defiling and snatching away the souls of maidens, in a London season.

I have no time to trace for you any more harpy legends, though they are full of the most curious interest; but I may confirm for you my interpretation of this one, and prove its importance in the Greek mind, by noting that Polygnotus painted these maidens, in his great religious series of paintings at Delphi, crowned with flowers, and playing at dice; and that Penelope remembers them in her last fit of despair, just before the return of Ulysses; and prays bitterly that she may be snatched away at once into nothingness by the Harpies, like Pandareos' daughters, rather than be tormented longer by her deferred hope, and anguish of disappointed love.

25. I have hitherto spoken only of deities of the winds. We pass now to a far more important group, the Deities of Cloud. Both of these are subordinate to the ruling power of the air, as the demigods of the fountains and minor seas are to the great deep: but, as the cloud-firmament detaches itself more from the air, and has a wider range of ministry than the minor streams and seas, the highest cloud deity, Hermes, has a rank more equal with Athena than Nereus or Proteus with Neptune; and there is greater difficulty in tracing his character, because his physical dominion over the clouds can, of course, be asserted only where clouds are; and, therefore, scarcely at all in Egypt:* so that the changes which Hermes undergoes in becoming a Greek from an Egyptian and Phœnician god, are greater than in any other case of adopted tradition. In Egypt Hermes is a deity of historical record, and a conductor of the dead to judgment; the Greeks take away much of this historical function, assigning it to the Muses; but, in investing him with the physical power over clouds, they give him that which the Muses disdain, the power of concealment, and of theft. The snatching away by the

---

* I believe that the conclusions of recent scholarship are generally opposed to the Herodotean ideas of any direct acceptance by the Greeks of Egyptian myths: and very certainly, Greek art is developed by giving the veracity and simplicity of real life to Eastern savage grotesque; and not by softening the severity of pure Egyptian design. But it is of no consequence whether one conception was, or was not, in this case, derived from the other; my object is only to mark the essential differences between them.

Harpies is with brute force; but the snatching away by the clouds is connected with the thought of hiding, and of making things seem to be what they are not; so that Hermes is the god of lying, as he is of mist; and yet with this ignoble function of making things vanish and disappear, is connected the remnant of his grand Egyptian authority of leading away souls in the cloud of death (the actual dimness of sight caused by mortal wounds physically suggesting the darkness and descent of clouds, and continually being so described in the Iliad); while the sense of the need of guidance on the untrodden road follows necessarily. You cannot but remember how this thought of cloud guidance, and cloud receiving of souls at death, has been elsewhere ratified.

26. Without following that higher clue, I will pass to the lovely group of myths connected with the birth of Hermes on the Greek mountains. You know that the valley of Sparta is one of the noblest mountain ravines in the world, and that the western flank of it is formed by an unbroken chain of crags, forty miles long, rising, opposite Sparta, to a height of 8,000 feet, and known as the chain of Taygetus. Now, the nymph from whom that mountain ridge is named, was the mother of Lacedæmon; therefore, the mythic ancestress of the Spartan race. She is the nymph Taygeta, and one of the seven stars of spring; one of those Pleiades of whom is the question to Job,— "Canst thou bind the sweet influences of Pleiades, or loose the bands of Orion?" "The sweet influences of Pleiades," of the stars of spring,—nowhere sweeter than among the

pine-clad slopes of the hills of Sparta and Arcadia, when the snows of their higher summits, beneath the sunshine of April, fell into fountains, and rose into clouds; and in every ravine was a newly-awakened voice of waters,— soft increase of whisper among its sacred stones : and on every crag its forming and fading veil of radiant cloud; temple above temple, of the divine marble that no tool can pollute, nor ruin undermine. And, therefore, beyond this central valley, this great Greek vase of Arcadia, on the "*hollow*" mountain, Cyllene, or " pregnant" mountain, called also " cold," because there the vapours rest,* and born of the eldest of those stars of spring, that Maia, from whom your own month of May has its name, bringing to you, in the green of her garlands, and the white of her hawthorn, the unrecognized symbols of the pastures and the wreathed snows of Arcadia, where long ago she was queen of stars : there, first cradled and wrapt in swaddling-clothes ; then raised, in a moment of surprise, into his wandering power,— is born the shepherd of the clouds, winged-footed and deceiving,—blinding the eyes of Argus,—escaping from the grasp of Apollo—restless messenger between the highest sky and topmost earth—"the herald Mercury, new lighted on a heaven-kissing hill."

27. Now, it will be wholly impossible, at present, to trace for you any of the minor Greek expressions of this thought, except only that Mercury, as the cloud shepherd,

* On the altar of Hermes on its summit, as on that of the Lacinian Hera, no wind ever stirred the ashes. By those altars, the Gods of Heaven were appeased ; and all their storms at rest.

is especially called Eriophoros, the wool-bearer. You will recollect the name from the common woolly rush "eriophorum" which has a cloud of silky seed; and note also that he wears distinctively the flat cap, *petasos*, named from a word meaning to expand; which shaded from the sun, and is worn on journeys. You have the epithet of mountains "cloud-capped" as an established form with every poet, and the Mont Pilate of Lucerne is named from a Latin word signifying specially a *woollen* cap; but Mercury has, besides, a general Homeric epithet, curiously and intensely concentrated in meaning, "the profitable or serviceable by wool," * that is to say, by shepherd wealth; hence, "pecuniarily," rich, or serviceable, and so he passes at last into a general mercantile deity; while yet the cloud sense of the wool is retained by Homer always, so that he gives him this epithet when it would otherwise have been quite meaningless, (in Iliad, xxiv. 440,) when he drives Priam's chariot, and breathes force into his horses, precisely as we shall find Athena drive Diomed: and yet the serviceable and profitable sense,—and something also of gentle and soothing character in the mere wool-softness, as used for dress, and religious rites,—is retained also in the epithet, and thus the gentle and serviceable Hermes is opposed to the deceitful one.

* I am convinced that the ἰοι in ἐριούνιος is not intensitive; but retained from ἴοιοι : but even if I am wrong in thinking this, the mistake is of no consequence with respect to the general force of the term as meaning the *profitableness* of Hermes. Athena's epithet of ἀγελεία has a parallel significance.

28. In connection with this driving of Priam's chariot, remember that as Autolycus is the son of Hermes the Deceiver, Myrtilus (the Auriga of the Stars) is the son of Hermes the Guide. The name Hermes itself means Impulse; and he is especially the shepherd of the flocks of the sky, in driving, or guiding, or stealing them; and yet his great name, Argeiphontes, not only—as in different passages of the olden poets—means "Shining White," which is said of him as being himself the silver cloud lighted by the sun; but "Argus-Killer," the killer of brightness, which is said of him as he veils the sky, and especially the stars, which are the eyes of Argus; or, literally, eyes of brightness, which Juno, who is, with Jupiter, part of the type of highest heaven, keeps in her peacock's train. We know that this interpretation is right, from a passage in which Euripides describes the shield of Hippomedon, which bore for its sign, "Argus the all-seeing, covered with eyes; open towards the rising of the stars, and closed towards their setting."

And thus Hermes becomes the spirit of the movement of the sky or firmament; not merely the fast flying of the transitory cloud, but the great motion of the heavens and stars themselves. Thus, in his highest power, he corresponds to the "primo mobile" of the later Italian philosophy, and, in his simplest, is the guide of all mysterious and cloudy movement, and of all successful subtleties. Perhaps the prettiest minor recognition of his character is when, on the night foray of Ulysses and Diomed, Ulysses wears the helmet stolen by Autolycus, the son of Hermes.

29. The position in the Greek mind of Hermes as the Lord of cloud is, however, more mystic and ideal than that of any other deity, just on account of the constant and real presence of the cloud itself under different forms, giving rise to all kinds of minor fables. The play of the Greek imagination in this direction is so wide and complex, that I cannot even give you an outline of its range in my present limits. There is first a great series of storm-legends connected with the family of the historic Æolus, centralized by the story of Athamas, with his two wives, "the Cloud" and the "White Goddess," ending in that of Phrixus and Helle, and of the golden fleece (which is only the cloud-burden of Hermes Eriophoros). With this, there is the fate of Salmoneus, and the destruction of Glaucus by his own horses; all these minor myths of storm concentrating themselves darkly into the legend of Bellerophon and the Chimæra, in which there is an under story about the vain subduing of passion and treachery, and the end of life in fading melancholy,—which, I hope, not many of you could understand even were I to show it you: (the merely physical meaning of the Chimæra is the cloud of volcanic lightning, connected wholly with earth-fire, but resembling the heavenly cloud in its height and its thunder). Finally, in the Æolic group, there is the legend of Sisyphus, which I mean to work out thoroughly by itself: its root is in the position of Corinth as ruling

the isthmus and the two seas—the Corinthian Acropolis, two thousand feet high, being the centre of the crossing currents of the winds, and ⁎of the commerce of Greece. Therefore, Athena, and the fountain cloud Pegasus, are more closely connected with Corinth than even with Athens in their material, though not in their moral power; and Sisyphus founds the Isthmian games in connection with a melancholy story about the sea gods; but he himself is κέρδιστος ἀνδρῶν, the most "gaining" and subtle of men; who, having the key of the Isthmus, becomes the type of transit, transfer, or trade, as such; and of the apparent gain from it, which is not gain: and this is the real meaning of his punishment in hell—eternal toil and recoil (the modern idol of capital being, indeed, the stone of Sisyphus with a vengeance, *crushing* in its recoil). But, throughout, the old ideas of the cloud power and cloud feebleness,—the deceit of its hiding,—and the emptiness of its vanishing,—the Autolycus enchantment of making black seem white,—and the disappointed fury of Ixion (taking shadow for power), mingle in the moral meaning of this and its collateral legends; and give an aspect, at last, not only of foolish cunning, but of impiety or literal "idolatry," "imagination worship," to the dreams of avarice and injustice, until this notion of atheism and insolent blindness becomes principal; and the "Clouds" of Aristophanes, with the personified "just" and "unjust" sayings in the latter part of the play, foreshadow, almost feature by feature, in all that they were written to mock and to chastise, the worst elements of the impious "δῖνος" and tumult in men's thoughts, which have followed on their avarice in the present day, making them alike forsake the laws of their ancient gods, and misapprehend or reject the true words of their existing teachers.

30. All this we have from the legends of the historic Æolus only; but, besides these, there is the beautiful story of Semele, the Mother of Bacchus. She is the cloud with the strength of the vine in its bosom, consumed by the light which matures the fruit; the melting away of the cloud into the clear air at the fringe of its edges being exquisitely rendered by Pindar's epithet for her, Semele, "with the stretched-out hair" (τανυέθειρα). Then there is the entire tradition of the Danaides, and of the tower of Danae and golden shower; the birth of Perseus connecting this legend with that of the Gorgons and Graiæ, who are the true clouds of thunderous and ruinous tempest. I must, in passing, mark for you that the form of the sword or sickle of Perseus, with which he kills Medusa, is another image of the whirling harpy vortex, and belongs especially to the sword of destruction or annihilation; whence it is given to the two angels who gather for destruction the evil harvest and evil vintage of the earth (Rev. xiv. 15). I will collect afterwards and complete what I have already written respecting the Pegasean and Gorgonian legends, noting here only what is necessary to explain the central myth of Athena herself, who represents the ambient air, which included all cloud, and rain, and dew, and dark-

ness, and peace, and wrath of heaven. Let me now try to give you, however briefly, some distinct idea of the several agencies of this great goddess.

31. I. She is the air giving life and health to all animals.
II. She is the air giving vegetative power to the earth.
III. She is the air giving motion to the sea, and rendering navigation possible.
IV. She is the air nourishing artificial light, torch or lamplight; as opposed to that of the sun, on one hand, and of *consuming* * fire on the other.
V. She is the air conveying vibration of sound.

I will give you instances of her agency in all these functions.

32. First, and chiefly, she is air as the spirit of life, giving vitality to the blood. Her psychic relation to the vital force in matter lies deeper, and we will examine it afterwards; but a great number of the most interesting passages in Homer regard her as flying over the earth in local and transitory strength, simply and merely the goddess of fresh air.

It is curious that the British city which has somewhat saucily styled itself the Modern Athens, is indeed more under her especial tutelage and favour in this respect than perhaps any other town in the island. Athena is first simply what in the Modern Athens you so practically

---

* Not a scientific, but a very practical and expressive distinction.

find her, the breeze of the mountain and the sea; and wherever she comes, there is purification, and health, and power. The sea-beach round this isle of ours is the frieze of our Parthenon : every wave that breaks on it thunders with Athena's voice ; nay, whenever you throw your window wide open in the morning, you let in Athena, as wisdom and fresh air at the same instant; and whenever you draw a pure, long, full breath of right heaven, you take Athena into your heart, through your blood; and, with the blood, into the thoughts of your brain.

Now this giving of strength by the air, observe, is mechanical as well as chemical. You cannot strike a good blow but with your chest full; and in hand to hand fighting, it is not the muscle that fails first, it is the breath; the longest-breathed will, on the average, be the victor,— not the strongest. Note how Shakspeare always leans on this. Of Mortimer, in "changing hardiment with great Glendower:"—

> "Three times they breathed, and three times did they drink,
> Upon agreement, of swift Severn's flood."

And again, Hotspur sending challenge to Prince Harry:—

> "That none might draw short breath to-day
> But I and Harry Monmouth."

Again, of Hamlet, before he receives his wound :—

> "He's fat, and scant of breath."

Again, Orlando in the wrestling :—

> "Yes; I beseech your grace
> I am not yet well breathed."

Now of all people that ever lived, the Greeks knew best

what breath meant, both in exercise and in battle; and therefore the queen of the air becomes to them at once the queen of bodily strength in war; not mere brutal muscular strength,—that belongs to Ares,—but the strength of young lives passed in pure air and swift exercise,— Camilla's virginal force, that " flies o'er the unbending corn, and skims along the main."

33. Now I will rapidly give you two or three instances of her direct agency in this function. First, when she wants to make Penelope bright and beautiful; and to do away with the signs of her waiting and her grief. " Then Athena thought of another thing; she laid her into deep sleep, and loosed all her limbs, and made her taller, and made her smoother, and fatter, and whiter than sawn ivory; and breathed ambrosial brightness over her face; and so she left her and went up to heaven." Fresh air and sound sleep at night, young ladies! You see you may have Athena for lady's maid whenever you choose. Next, hark how she gives strength to Achilles when he is broken with fasting and grief. Jupiter pities him and says to her,—" ' Daughter mine, are you forsaking your own soldier, and don't you care for Achilles any more? see how hungry and weak he is,—go and feed him with ambrosia.' So he urged the eager Athena; and she leaped down out of heaven like a harpy falcon, shrill voiced; and she poured nectar and ambrosia, full of delight, into the breast of Achilles, that his limbs might not fail with famine: then she returned to the solid dome of her strong father." And then comes the great passage about Achilles

arming—for which we have no time. But here is again Athena giving strength to the whole Greek army. She came as a falcon to Achilles, straight at him;—a sudden drift of breeze; but to the army she must come widely,—she sweeps round them all. "As when Jupiter spreads the purple rainbow over heaven, portending battle or cold storm, so Athena, wrapping herself round with a purple cloud, stooped to the Greek soldiers, and raised up each of them." Note that purple, in Homer's use of it, nearly always means "fiery," "full of light." It is the light of the rainbow, not the colour of it, which Homer means you to think of.

34. But the most curious passage of all, and fullest of meaning, is when she gives strength to Menelaus, that he may stand unwearied against Hector. He prays to her: "And blue-eyed Athena was glad that he prayed to her, first; and she gave him strength in his shoulders, and in his limbs, and she gave him the courage"—of what animal, do you suppose? Had it been Neptune or Mars, they would have given him the courage of a bull, or a lion; but Athena gives him the courage of the most fearless in attack of all creatures—small or great—and very small it is, but wholly incapable of terror,—she gives him the courage of a fly.

35. Now this simile of Homer's is one of the best instances I can give you of the way in which great writers seize truths unconsciously which are for all time. It is only recent science which has completely shown the perfectness of this minute symbol of the power of Athena;

proving that the insect's flight and breath are co-ordinated; that its wings are actually forcing-pumps, of which the stroke compels the thoracic respiration; and that it thus breathes and flies simultaneously by the action of the same muscles, so that respiration is carried on most vigorously during flight, " while the air-vessels, supplied by many pairs of lungs instead of one, traverse the organs of flight in far greater numbers than the capillary blood-vessels of our own system, and give enormous and untiring muscular power, a rapidity of action measured by thousands of strokes in the minute, and an endurance, by miles and hours of flight." *

Homer could not have known this; neither that the buzzing of the fly was produced as in a wind instrument, by a constant current of air through the trachea. But he had seen, and, doubtless, meant us to remember, the marvellous strength and swiftness of the insect's flight (the glance of the swallow itself is clumsy and slow compared to the darting of common house-flies at play); he probably attributed its murmur to the wings, but in this also there was a type of what we shall presently find recognized in the name of Pallas,—the vibratory power of the air to convey sound,—while, as a purifying creature, the fly holds its place beside the old symbol of Athena in Egypt, the vulture; and as a venomous and tormenting creature, has more than the strength of the serpent in proportion to its size, being thus entirely representative of the influence of

* Ormerod. *Natural History of Wasps*.

the air both in purification and pestilence ; and its courage is so notable that, strangely enough, forgetting Homer's simile, I happened to take the fly for an expression of the audacity of freedom in speaking of quite another subject.*
Whether it should be called courage, or mere mechanical instinct, may be questioned, but assuredly no other animal, exposed to continual danger, is so absolutely without sign of fear.

36. You will, perhaps, have still patience to hear two instances, not of the communication of strength, but of the personal agency of Athena as the air. When she comes down to help Diomed against Ares, she does not come to fight instead of him, but she takes his charioteer's place.

> "She snatched the reins, she lashed with all her force,
> And full on Mars impelled the foaming horse."

Ares is the first to cast his spear; then, note this, Pope says:—

> "Pallas opposed her hand, and caused to glance,
> Far from the car, the strong immortal lance."

She does not oppose her hand in the Greek—the wind could not meet the lance straight—she catches it in her hand, and throws it off. There is no instance in which a lance is so parried by a mortal hand in all the Iliad, and it is exactly the way the wind would parry it, catching it, and turning it aside. If there are any good rifleshots here —they know something about Athena's parrying—and in old times the English masters of feathered artillery knew

* See farther on, § 148, pp 152–153.

more yet. Compare also the turning of Hector's lance from Achilles : Iliad xx. 439.

37. The last instance I will give you is as lovely as it is subtle. Throughout the Iliad, Athena is herself the will or Menis of Achilles. If he is to be calmed, it is she who calms him ; if angered, it is she who inflames him. In the first quarrel with Atrides, when he stands at pause, with the great sword half drawn, " Athena came from heaven, and stood behind him, and caught him by the yellow hair." Another god would have stayed his hand upon the hilt, but Athena only lifts his hair. " And he turned and knew her, and her dreadful eyes shone upon him." There is an exquisite tenderness in this laying her hand upon his hair, for it is the talisman of his life, vowed to his own Thessalian river if he ever returned to its shore, and cast upon Patroclus' pile, so ordaining that there should be no return.

38. Secondly—Athena is the air giving vegetative impulse to the earth. She is the wind and the rain—and yet more the pure air itself, getting at the earth fresh turned by spade or plough—and, above all, feeding the fresh leaves; for though the Greeks knew nothing about carbonic acid, they did know that trees fed on the air.

Now, note first in this, the myth of the air getting at ploughed ground. You know I told you the Lord of all labour by which man lived was Hephæstus; therefore Athena adopts a child of his, and of the Earth,—Erichthonius,—literally, " the tearer up of the ground "—who is the head (though not in direct line,) of the kings of Attica ; and having adopted him, she gives him to be brought up by the three nymphs of the dew. Of these, Aglauros, the dweller in the fields, is the envy or malice of the earth ; she answers nearly to the envy of Cain, the tiller of the ground, against his shepherd brother, in her own envy against her two sisters, Herse, the cloud dew, who is the beloved of the shepherd Mercury ; and Pandrosos, the diffused dew, or dew of heaven. Literally, you have in this myth the words of the blessing of Esau—. " Thy dwelling shall be of the fatness of the earth, and of the dew of heaven from above." Aglauros is for her envy turned into a black stone ; and hers is one of the voices,— the other being that of Cain,—which haunts the circle of envy in the Purgatory :—

"Io sono Aglauro, chi divenne sasso."

But to her two sisters, with Erichthonius, (or the hero Erectheus,) is built the most sacred temple of Athena in Athens ; the temple to their own dearest Athena—to her, and to the dew together : so that it was divided into two parts : one, the temple of Athena of the city, and the other that of the dew. And this expression of her power, as the air bringing the dew to the hill pastures, in the central temple of the central city of the heathen, dominant over the future intellectual world, is, of all the facts connected with her worship as the spirit of life, perhaps the most important. I have no time now to trace for you the hundredth part of the different ways in which it bears both upon natural beauty, and on the best order and happiness of men's lives. I hope to follow out some of these trains of thought in gathering together what I have to say about field herbage; but I must say briefly here that the great sign, to the Greeks, of the coming of spring in the pastures, was not, as with us, in the primrose, but in the various flowers of the asphodel tribe (of which I will give you some separate account presently); therefore it is that the earth answers with crocus flame to the cloud on Ida; and the power of Athena in eternal life is written by the light of the asphodel on the Elysian fields.

But farther, Athena is the air, not only to the lilies of the field, but to the leaves of the forest. We saw before the reason why Hermes is said to be the son of Maia, the eldest of the sister stars of spring. Those stars are called not only Pleiades, but Vergiliæ, from a word mingling the ideas of the turning or returning of spring-time with the outpouring of rain. The mother of Virgil bearing the name of Maia, Virgil himself received his name from the seven stars; and he, in forming, first, the mind of Dante, and through him that of Chaucer (besides whatever special minor influence came from the Pastorals and Georgics), became the fountain-head of all the best literary power connected with the love of vegetative nature among civilized races of men. Take the fact for what it is worth; still it is a strange seal of coincidence, in word and in reality, upon the Greek dream of the power over human life, and its purest thoughts, in the stars of spring. But the first syllable of the name of Virgil has relation also to another group of words, of which the English ones, virtue, and virgin, bring down the force to modern days. It is a group containing mainly the idea of " spring," or increase of life in vegetation—the rising of the new branch of the tree out of the bud, and of the new leaf out of the ground. It involves, secondarily, the idea of greenness and of strength, but primarily, that of living increase of a new rod from a stock, stem, or root ; ("There shall come forth a rod out of the stem of Jesse;") and chiefly the stem of certain plants—either of the rose tribe, as in the budding of the almond rod of Aaron ; or of the olive tribe, which has triple significance in this symbolism, from the use of its oil for sacred anointing, for strength in the gymnasium, and for light. Hence, in numberless divided and reflected ways, it is connected with the power of Hercules and Athena: Hercules plants the wild olive, for its shade, on the course of Olympia, and it thenceforward gives the Olympic crown, of consummate honour and rest; while the prize at the Panathenaic games is a vase of its oil, (meaning encouragement to continuance of effort); and from the paintings on these Panathenaic vases we get the most precious clue to the entire character of Athena. Then to express its propagation by slips, the trees from which the oil was to be taken were called "Moriai," trees of division (being all descendants of the sacred one in the Erechtheum). And thus, in one direction, we get to the "children like olive plants round about thy table" and the olive grafting of St. Paul; while the use of the oil for anointing gives chief name to the rod itself of the stem of Jesse, and to all those who were by that name signed for his disciples first in Antioch. Remember, farther, since that name was first given, the influence of the symbol, both in extreme unction, and in consecration of priests and kings to their "divine right;" and think, if you can reach with any grasp of thought, what the influence on the earth has been, of those twisted branches whose leaves give grey bloom to the hill-sides under every breeze that blows from the midland sea. But, above and beyond all, think how strange it is that the chief Agonia of humanity, and the chief giving of strength from heaven for its fulfilment, should have been under its night shadow in Palestine.

39. Thirdly—Athena is the air in its power over the sea.

On the earliest Panathenaic vase known—the "Burgon" vase in the British Museum—Athena has a dolphin on her shield. The dolphin has two principal meanings in Greek symbolism. It means, first, the sea; secondarily, the ascending and descending course of any of the heavenly bodies from one sea horizon to another—the dolphins' arching rise and replunge (in a summer evening, out of calm sea, their black backs roll round with exactly the slow motion of a water-wheel; but I do not know how far Aristotle's exaggerated account of their leaping or their swiftness has any foundation,) being taken as a type of the emergence of the sun or stars from the sea in the east, and plunging beneath in the west. Hence, Apollo, when in his personal power he crosses the sea, leading his Cretan colonists to Pytho, takes the form of a dolphin, becomes Apollo Delphinius, and names the founded colony "Delphi." The lovely drawing of the Delphic Apollo on the hydria of the Vatican (Le Normand and De Witte, vol. ii. p. 6), gives the entire conception of this myth. Again, the beautiful coins of Tarentum represent Taras coming to found the city, riding on a dolphin, whose leaps and plunges have partly the rage of the sea in them, and partly the spring of the horse, because the splendid riding of the Tarentines had made their name proverbial in Magna Græcia. The story of Arion is a collateral fragment of the same thought; and, again, the plunge before their transformation, of the ships of Æneas. Then, this idea of career upon, or conquest of the sea, either by the creatures themselves, or by dolphin-like ships, (compare the Merlin prophecy,—

"They shall ride
Over ocean wide
With hempen bridle, and horse of tree,)"

connects itself with the thought of undulation, and of the wave-power in the sea itself, which is always expressed by the serpentine bodies either of the sea-gods or of the sea-horse; and when Athena carries, as she does often in later work, a serpent for her shield-sign, it is not so much the repetition of her own ægis-snakes as the farther expression of her power over the sea-wave; which, finally, Virgil gives in its perfect unity with her own anger, in the approach of the serpents against Laocoon from the sea;

and then, finally, when her own storm-power is fully put forth on the ocean also, and the madness of the ægis-snake is given to the wave-snake, the sea-wave becomes the devouring hound at the waist of Scylla, and Athena takes Scylla for her helmet-crest; while yet her beneficent and essential power on the ocean, in making navigation possible, is commemorated in the Panathenaic festival by her peplus being carried to the Erechtheum suspended from the mast of a ship.

In Plate cxv. of vol. ii., Le Normand, are given two sides of a vase, which, in rude and childish way, assembles most of the principal thoughts regarding Athena in this relation. In the first, the sunrise is represented by the ascending chariot of Apollo, foreshortened; the light is supposed to blind the eyes, and no face of the god is seen (Turner, in the Ulysses and Polyphemus sunrise, loses the form of the god in light, giving the chariot-horses only; rendering in his own manner, after 2,200 years of various fall and revival of the arts, precisely the same thought as the old Greek potter). He ascends out of the sea; but the sea itself has not yet caught the light. In the second design, Athena as the morning breeze, and Hermes as the morning cloud, fly over the sea before the sun. Hermes turns back his head; his face is unseen in the cloud, as Apollo's in the light; the grotesque appearance of an animal's face is only the cloud-phantasm modifying a frequent form of the hair of Hermes beneath the back of his cap. Under the morning breeze, the dolphins leap from the rippled sea, and their sides catch the light.

The coins of the Lucanian Heracleia give a fair representation of the helmed Athena, as imagined in later Greek art, with the embossed Scylla.

40. Fourthly—Athena is the air nourishing artificial light—unconsuming fire. Therefore, a lamp was always kept burning in the Erechtheum; and the torch-race belongs chiefly to her festival, of which the meaning is to show the danger of the perishing of the light even by excess of the air that nourishes it: and so that the race is not to the swift, but to the wise. The household use of her constant light is symbolized in the lovely passage in the Odyssey, where Ulysses and his son move the armour while the servants are shut in their chambers, and there is no one to hold torches for them; but Athena herself, "having a golden lamp," fills all the rooms with light. Her presence in war-strength with her favourite heroes is always shown by the "unwearied" fire hovering on their helmets and shields; and the image gradually becomes constant and accepted, both for the maintenance of household watchfulness, as in the parable of the ten virgins, or as the symbol of direct inspiration, in the rushing wind and divided flames of Pentecost: but, together with this thought of unconsuming and constant fire, there is always mingled in the Greek mind the sense of the consuming by excess, as of the flame by the air, so also of the inspired creature by its own fire (thus, again, "the zeal of thine house hath eaten me up"—"my zeal hath consumed me, because of thine enemies," and the like); and especially

Athena has this aspect towards the truly sensual and bodily strength; so that to Ares, who is himself insane and consuming, the opposite wisdom seems to be insane and consuming: "All we the other gods have thee against us, O Jove! when we would give grace to men; for thou hast begotten the maid without a mind—the mischievous creature, the doer of unseemly evil. All we obey thee, and are ruled by thee. Her only thou wilt not resist in anything she says or does, because thou didst bear her—consuming child as she is."

41. Lastly—Athena is the air, conveying vibration of sound.

In all the loveliest representations in central Greek art of the birth of Athena, Apollo stands close to the sitting Jupiter, singing, with a deep, quiet joyfulness, to his lyre. The sun is always thought of as the master of time and rhythm, and as the origin of the composing and inventive discovery of melody; but the air, as the actual element and substance of the voice, the prolonging and sustaining power of it, and the symbol of its moral passion. Whatever in music is measured and designed, belongs therefore to Apollo and the Muses; whatever is impulsive and passionate, to Athena: hence her constant strength of voice or cry (as when she aids the shout of Achilles) curiously opposed to the dumbness of Demeter. The Apolline lyre, therefore, is not so much the instrument producing sound, as its measurer and divider by length or tension of string into given notes; and I believe it is, in a double connection with its office as a measurer of time or motion, and its relation to the transit of the sun in the sky, that Hermes forms it from the tortoise-shell, which is the image of the dappled concave of the cloudy sky. Thenceforward all the limiting or restraining modes of music belong to the Muses; but the passionate music is wind music, as in the Doric flute. Then, when this inspired music becomes degraded in its passion, it sinks into the pipe of Pan, and the double pipe of Marsyas, and is then rejected by Athena. The myth which represents her doing so is that she invented the double pipe from hearing the hiss of the Gorgonian serpents; but when she played upon it, chancing to see her face reflected in water, she saw that it was distorted, whereupon she threw down the flute, which Marsyas found. Then, the strife of Apollo and Marsyas represents the enduring contest between music in which the words and thought lead, and the lyre measures or melodizes them, (which Pindar means when he calls his hymns "kings over the lyre,") and music in which the words are lost, and the wind or impulse leads,—generally, therefore, between intellectual, and brutal, or meaningless, music. Therefore, when Apollo prevails, he flays Marsyas, taking the limit and external bond of his shape from him, which is death, without touching the mere muscular strength; yet shameful and dreadful in dissolution.

42. And the opposition of these two kinds of sound is continually dwelt upon by the Greek philosophers, the real fact at the root of all their teaching being this,—that

true music is the natural expression of a lofty passion for a right cause; that in proportion to the kingliness and force of any personality, the expression either of its joy or suffering becomes measured, chastened, calm, and capable of interpretation only by the majesty of ordered, beautiful, and worded sound. Exactly in proportion to the degree in which we become narrow in the cause and conception of our passions, incontinent in the utterance of them, feeble of perseverance in them, sullied or shameful in the indulgence of them, their expression by musical sound becomes broken, mean, fatuitous, and at last impossible; the measured waves of the air of heaven will not lend themselves to expression of ultimate vice, it must be for ever sunk into discordance or silence. And since, as before stated, every work of right art has a tendency to reproduce the ethical state which first developed it, this, which of all the arts is most directly ethical in origin, is also the most direct in power of discipline; the first, the simplest, the most effective of all instruments of moral instruction; while in the failure and betrayal of its functions, it becomes the subtlest aid of moral degradation. Music is thus, in her health, the teacher of perfect order, and is the voice of the obedience of angels, and the companion of the course of the spheres of heaven; and in her depravity she is also the teacher of perfect disorder and disobedience, and the Gloria in Excelsis becomes the Marseillaise. In the third section of this volume, I reprint two chapters from another essay of mine, (" The Cestus of Aglaia,") on modesty or measure, and on liberty, containing farther reference to music in her two powers; and I do this now, because, among the many monstrous and misbegotten fantasies which are the spawn of modern licence, perhaps the most impishly opposite to the truth is the conception of music which has rendered possible the writing, by educated persons, and, more strangely yet, the tolerant criticism, of such words as these: —" *This so persuasive art is the only one that has no didactic efficacy, that engenders no emotions save such as are without issue on the side of moral truth, that expresses nothing of God, nothing of reason, nothing of human liberty.*" I will not give the author's name; the passage is quoted in the *Westminster Review* for last January, p. 153.

43. I must also anticipate something of what I have to say respecting the relation of the power of Athena to organic life, so far as to note that her name, Pallas, probably refers to the quivering or vibration of the air; and to its power, whether as vital force, or communicated wave, over every kind of matter, in giving it vibratory movement; first, and most intense, in the voice and throat of the bird; which is the air incarnate; and so descending through the various orders of animal life to the vibrating and semi-voluntary murmur of the insect; and, lower still, to the hiss, or quiver of the tail, of the half-lunged snake and deaf adder; all these, nevertheless, being wholly under the rule of Athena as representing either breath, or vital nervous power; and, therefore, also, in their simplicity, the " oaten

pipe and pastoral song," which belong to her dominion over the asphodel meadows, and breathe on their banks of violets.

Finally, is it not strange to think of the influence of this one power of Pallas in vibration; (we shall see a singular mechanical energy of it presently in the serpent's motion;) in the voices of war and peace? How much of the repose—how much of the wrath, folly, and misery of men, has literally depended on this one power of the air;—on the sound of the trumpet and of the bell—on the lark's song, and the bee's murmur.

44. Such is the general conception in the Greek mind of the physical power of Athena. The spiritual power associated with it is of two kinds;—first, she is the Spirit of Life in material organism; not strength in the blood only, but formative energy in the clay: and, secondly, she is inspired and impulsive wisdom in human conduct and human art, giving the instinct of infallible decision, and of faultless invention.

It is quite beyond the scope of my present purpose—and, indeed, will only be possible for me at all after marking the relative intention of the Apolline myths—to trace for you the Greek conception of Athena as the guide of moral passion. But I will at least endeavor, on some near occasion,* to define some of the actual truths respecting the vital force in created organism, and inventive fancy in the

* I have tried to do this in mere outline in the two following sections of this volume.

works of man, which are more or less expressed by the Greeks, under the personality of Athena. You would, perhaps, hardly bear with me if I endeavoured farther to show you—what is nevertheless perfectly true—the analogy between the spiritual power of Athena in her gentle ministry, yet irresistible anger, with the ministry of another Spirit whom we also, holding for the universal power of life, are forbidden, at our worst peril, to quench or to grieve.

45. But, I think, to-night, you should not let me close, without requiring of me an answer on one vital point, namely, how far these imaginations of Gods—which are vain to us—were vain to those who had no better trust? and what real belief the Greek had in these creations of his own spirit, practical and helpful to him in the sorrow of earth? I am able to answer you explicitly in this. The origin of his thoughts is often obscure, and we may err in endeavouring to account for their form of realization; but the effect of that realization on his life is not obscure at all. The Greek creed was, of course, different in its character, as our own creed is, according to the class of persons who held it. The common people's was quite literal, simple, and happy: their idea of Athena was as clear as a good Roman Catholic peasant's idea of the Madonna. In Athens itself, the centre of thought and refinement, Pisistratus obtained the reins of government through the ready belief of the populace that a beautiful woman, armed like Athena, was the goddess

herself. Even at the close of the last century some of this simplicity remained among the inhabitants of the Greek islands; and when a pretty English lady first made her way into the grotto of Antiparos, she was surrounded, on her return, by all the women of the neighbouring village, believing her to be divine, and praying her to heal them of their sicknesses.

46. Then, secondly, the creed of the upper classes was more refined and spiritual, but quite as honest, and even more forcible in its effect on the life. You might imagine that the employment of the artifice just referred to implied utter unbelief in the persons contriving it; but it really meant only that the more worldly of them would play with a popular faith for their own purposes, as doubly-minded persons have often done since, all the while sincerely holding the same ideas themselves in a more abstract form; while the good and unworldly men, the true Greek heroes, lived by their faith as firmly as St. Louis, or the Cid, or the Chevalier Bayard.

47. Then, thirdly, the faith of the poets and artists was, necessarily, less definite, being continually modified by the involuntary action of their own fancies; and by the necessity of presenting, in clear verbal or material form, things of which they had no authoritative knowledge. Their faith was, in some respects, like Dante's or Milton's: firm in general conception, but not able to vouch for every detail in the forms they gave it: but they went considerably farther, even in that minor sincerity, than subsequent

poets; and strove with all their might to be as near the truth as they could. Pindar says, quite simply, "I cannot think so-and-so of the Gods. It must have been this way—it cannot have been that way—that the thing was done." And as late among the Latins as the days of Horace, this sincerity remains. Horace is just as true and simple in his religion as Wordsworth; but all power of understanding any of the honest classic poets has been taken away from most English gentlemen by the mechanical drill in verse-writing at school. Throughout the whole of their lives afterwards, they never can get themselves quit of the notion that all verses were written as an exercise, and that Minerva was only a convenient word for the last of an hexameter, and Jupiter for the last but one.

48. It is impossible that any notion can be more fallacious or more misleading in its consequences. All great song, from the first day when human lips contrived syllables, has been sincere song. With deliberate didactic purpose the tragedians—with pure and native passion the lyrists—fitted their perfect words to their dearest faiths. "Operosa parvus carmina fingo." "I, little thing that I am, weave my laborious songs" as earnestly as the bee among the bells of thyme on the Matin mountains. Yes, and he dedicates his favourite pine to Diana, and he chants his autumnal hymn to the Faun that guards his fields, and he guides the noble youths and maids of Rome in their choir to Apollo, and he tells the farmer's little girl

that the Gods will love her, though she has only a handful of salt and meal to give them—just as earnestly as ever English gentleman taught Christian faith to English youth, in England's truest days.

49. Then, lastly, the creed of the philosophers or sages varied according to the character and knowledge of each; —their relative acquaintance with the secrets of natural science — their intellectual and sectarian egotism — and their mystic or monastic tendencies, for there is a classic as well as a mediæval monasticism. They ended in losing the life of Greece in play upon words; but we owe to their early thought some of the soundest ethics, and the foundation of the best practical laws, yet known to mankind.

50. Such was the general vitality of the heathen creed in its strength. Of its direct influence on conduct, it is, as I said, impossible for me to speak now; only, remember always, in endeavouring to form a judgment of it, that what of good or right the heathens did, they did looking for no reward. The purest forms of our own religion have always consisted in sacrificing less things to win greater;— time, to win eternity,—the world, to win the skies. The order, "sell that thou hast," is not given without the promise,—"thou shalt have treasure in heaven;" and well for the modern Christian if he accepts the alternative as his Master left it—and does not practically read the command and promise thus: "Sell that thou hast in the best market, and thou shalt have treasure in eternity also."

But the poor Greeks of the great ages expected no reward from heaven but honour, and no reward from earth but rest;—though, when, on those conditions, they patiently, and proudly, fulfilled their task of the granted day, an unreasoning instinct of an immortal benediction broke from their lips in song: and they, even they, had sometimes a prophet to tell them of a land "where there is sun alike by day, and alike by night—where they shall need no more to trouble the earth by strength of hands for daily bread—but the ocean breezes blow around the blessed islands, and golden flowers burn on their bright trees for evermore."

II.

ATHENA KERAMITIS.*

(*Athena in the Earth.*)

Study, supplementary to the preceding lecture, of the supposed, and actual, relations of Athena to the vital force in material organism.

51. It has been easy to decipher approximately the Greek conception of the physical power of Athena in cloud and sky, because we know ourselves what clouds and skies are, and what the force of the wind is in forming them. But it is not at all easy to trace the Greek thoughts about the power of Athena in giving life, because we do not ourselves know clearly what life is, or in what way the air is necessary to it, or what there is, besides the air, shaping the forms that it is put into. And it is comparatively of small consequence to find out what the Greeks thought or meant, until we have determined what we ourselves think, or mean, when we translate the Greek word for "breathing" into the Latin-English word "spirit."

52. But it is of great consequence that you should fix in your minds—and hold, against the baseness of mere

---

* "Athena, fit for being made into pottery." I coin the expression as a counterpart of γῆ παρθένια, "Clay intact."

materialism on the one hand, and against the fallacies of controversial speculation on the other—the certain and practical sense of this word "spirit;"—the sense in which you all know that its reality exists, as the power which shaped you into your shape, and by which you love, and hate, when you have received that shape. You need not fear, on the one hand, that either the sculpturing or the loving power can ever be beaten down by the philosophers into a metal, or evolved by them into a gas: but, on the other hand, take care that you yourselves, in trying to elevate your conception of it, do not lose its truth in a dream, or even in a word. Beware always of contending for words: you will find them not easy to grasp, if you know them in several languages. This very word, which is so solemn in your mouths, is one of the most doubtful. In Latin it means little more than breathing, and may mean merely accent; in French it is not breath, but wit, and our neighbours are therefore obliged, even in their most solemn expressions, to say "wit" when we say "ghost." In Greek, "pneuma," the word we translate "ghost," means either wind or breath, and the relative word "psyche" has, perhaps, a more subtle power; yet St. Paul's words "pneumatic body" and "psychic body" involve a difference in his mind which no words will explain. But in Greek and in English, and in Saxon and in Hebrew, and in every articulate tongue of humanity, the "spirit of man" truly means his passion and virtue, and is stately according to the height of his conception, and stable according to the measure of his endurance.

53. Endurance, or patience, that is the central sign of spirit; a constancy against the cold and agony of death; and as, physically, it is by the burning power of the air that the heat of the flesh is sustained, so this Athena, spiritually, is the queen of all glowing virtue, the unconsuming fire and inner lamp of life. And thus, as Hephæstus is lord of the fire of the hand, and Apollo of the fire of the brain, so Athena of the fire of the heart; and as Hercules wears for his chief armour the skin of the Nemean lion, his chief enemy, whom he slew; and Apollo has for his highest name " the Pythian," from his chief enemy, the Python, slain; so Athena bears always on her breast the deadly face of her chief enemy slain, the Gorgonian cold, and venomous agony, that turns living men to stone.

54. And so long as you have that fire of the heart within you, and know the reality of it, you need be under no alarm as to the possibility of its chemical or mechanical analysis. The philosophers are very humorous in their ecstasy of hope about it; but the real interest of their discoveries in this direction is very small to human-kind. It is quite true that the tympanum of the ear vibrates under sound, and that the surface of the water in a ditch vibrates too: but the ditch hears nothing for all that; and my hearing is still to me as blessed a mystery as ever, and the interval between the ditch and me, quite as great. If the trembling sound in my ears was once of the marriage-bell which began my happiness, and is now of the passing-bell which ends it, the difference between those two sounds to

me cannot be counted by the number of concussions. There have been some curious speculations lately as to the conveyance of mental consciousness by "brain-waves." What does it matter how it is conveyed? The consciousness itself is not a wave. It may be accompanied here or there by any quantity of quivers and shakes, up or down, of anything you can find in the universe that is shakeable—what is that to me? My friend is dead, and my—according to modern views—vibratory sorrow is not one whit less, or less mysterious, to me, than my old quiet one.

55. Beyond, and entirely unaffected by, any questionings of this kind, there are, therefore, two plain facts which we should all know: first, that there is a power which gives their several shapes to things, or capacities of shape; and, secondly, a power which gives them their several feelings, or capacities of feeling; and that we can increase or destroy both of these at our will. By care and tenderness, we can extend the range of lovely life in plants and animals; by our neglect and cruelty, we can arrest it, and bring pestilence in its stead. Again, by right discipline we can increase our strength of noble will and passion, or destroy both. And whether these two forces are local conditions of the elements in which they appear, or are part of a great force in the universe, out of which they are taken, and to which they must be restored, is not of the slightest importance to us in dealing with them; neither is the manner of their connection with light and air. What precise meaning we ought to attach to expressions

such as that of the prophecy to the four winds that the dry bones might be breathed upon, and might live, or why the presence of the vital power should be dependent on the chemical action of the air, and its awful passing away materially signified by the rendering up of that breath or ghost, we cannot at present know, and need not at any time dispute. What we assuredly know is that the states of life and death are different, and the first more desirable than the other, and by effort attainable, whether we understand being " born of the spirit " to signify having the breath of heaven in our flesh, or its power in our hearts.

56. As to its power on the body, I will endeavor to tell you, having been myself much led into studies involving necessary reference both to natural science and mental phenomena, what, at least, remains to us after science has done its worst;—what the Myth of Athena, as a Formative and Decisive power—a Spirit of Creation and Volition, must eternally mean for all of us.

57. It is now (I believe I may use the strong word) " ascertained " that heat and motion are fixed in quantity, and measurable in the portions that we deal with. We can measure out portions of power, as we can measure portions of space; while yet, as far as we know, space may be infinite, and force infinite. There may be heat as much greater than the sun's, as the sun's heat is greater than a candle's; and force as much greater than the force by which the world swings, as that is greater than the force by which a cobweb trembles. Now, on heat and force,

life is inseparably dependent; and I believe, also, on a form of substance, which the philosophers call "protoplasm." I wish they would use English instead of Greek words. When I want to know why a leaf is green, they tell me it is coloured by "chlorophyll," which at first sounds very instructive; but if they would only say plainly that a leaf is coloured green by a thing which is called "green leaf," we should see more precisely how far we had got. However, it is a curious fact that life is connected with a cellular structure called protoplasm, or, in English, "first stuck together:" whence, conceivably through deuteroplasms, or second stickings, and tritoplasms, or third stickings,* we reach the highest plastic phase in the human pottery, which differs from common chinaware, primarily, by a measurable degree of heat, developed in breathing, which it borrows from the rest of the universe while it lives, and which it as certainly returns to the rest of the universe, when it dies.

58. Again, with this heat certain assimilative powers are connected, which the tendency of recent discovery is to

* Or, perhaps, we may be indulged with one consummating gleam of "glycasm" — visible "Sweetness," — according to the good old monk "Full moon," or "All moonshine." I cannot get at his original Greek, but am content with M. Durand's clear French (Manuel d'Iconographie Chrétienne. Paris, 1845):—" Lorsque vous aurez fait le proplasme, et esquissé un visage, vous ferez les chairs avec le glycasmo dont nous avons donné la recette. Chez les vieillards, vous indiquerez les rides, et chez les jeunes gens, les angles des yeux. C'est ainsi quo l'on fait les chairs, suivant Panselinos."

simplify more and more into modes of one force ; or finally into mere motion, communicable in various states, but not destructible. We will assume that science has done its utmost ; and that every chemical or animal force is demonstrably resolvable into heat or motion, reciprocally changing into each other. I would myself like better, in order of thought, to consider motion as a mode of heat than heat as a mode of motion : still, granting that we have got thus far, we have yet to ask, What is heat? or what motion? What is this "primo mobile," this transitional power, in which all things live, and move, and have their being? It is by definition something different from matter, and we may call it as we choose—"first cause," or "first light," or "first heat ;" but we can show no scientific proof of its not being personal, and coinciding with the ordinary conception of a supporting spirit in all things.

59. Still, it is not advisable to apply the word "spirit" or "breathing" to it, while it is only enforcing chemical affinities; but, when the chemical affinities are brought under the influence of the air, and of the sun's heat, the formative force enters an entirely different phase. It does not now merely crystallize indefinite masses, but it gives to limited portions of matter the power of gathering, selectively, other elements proper to them, and binding these elements into their own peculiar and adopted form.

This force, now properly called life, or breathing, or spirit, is continually creating its own shells of definite shape out of the wreck round it : and this is what I meant by saying, in the "Ethics of the Dust:"—"you may always stand by form against force." For the mere force of junction is not spirit; but the power that catches out of chaos charcoal, water, lime, or what not and fastens them down into a given form, is properly called "spirit;" and we shall not diminish, but strengthen our conception of this creative energy by recognizing its presence in lower states of matter than our own;—such recognition being enforced upon us by a delight we instinctively receive from all the forms of matter which manifest it; and yet more, by the glorifying of those forms, in the parts of them that are most animated, with the colours that are pleasantest to our senses. The most familiar instance of this is the best, and also the most wonderful: the blossoming of plants.

60. The Spirit in the plant,—that is to say, its power of gathering dead matter out of the wreck round it, and shaping it into its own chosen shape,—is of course strongest at the moment of its flowering, for it then not only gathers, but forms, with the greatest energy.

And where this Life is in it at full power, its form becomes invested with aspects that are chiefly delightful to our own human passions; namely, first, with the loveliest outlines of shape; and, secondly, with the most brilliant phases of the primary colours, blue, yellow, and red or white, the unison of all; and, to make it all more strange, this time of peculiar and perfect glory is associated with relations of the plants or blossoms to each other, correspondent to the joy of love in human creatures, and having the same object in the continuance of the race. Only, with respect to plants, as animals, we are wrong in speaking as if the object of this strong life were only the bequeathing of itself. The flower is the end or proper object of the seed, not the seed of the flower. The reason for seeds is that flowers may be; not the reason of flowers that seeds may be. The flower itself is the creature which the spirit makes; only, in connection with its perfectness, is placed the giving birth to its successor.

61. The main fact, then, about a flower is that it is the part of the plant's form developed at the moment of its intensest life: and this inner rapture is usually marked externally for us by the flush of one or more of the primary colours. What the character of the flower shall be, depends entirely upon the portion of the plant into which this rapture of spirit has been put. Sometimes the life is put into its outer sheath, and then the outer sheath becomes white and pure, and full of strength and grace; sometimes the life is put into the common leaves, just under the blossom, and they become scarlet or purple; sometimes the life is put into the stalks of the flower, and they flush blue; sometimes into its outer enclosure or calyx; mostly into its inner cup; but, in all cases, the presence of the strongest life is asserted by characters in which the human sight takes pleasure, and which seem prepared with distinct reference to us, or rather, bear, in being delightful, evidence of having been produced by the power of the same spirit as our own.

62. And we are led to feel this still more strongly, because all the distinctions of species,* both in plants and animals, appear to have similar connection with human character. Whatever the origin of species may be, or however those species, once formed, may be influenced by external accident, the groups into which birth or accident reduce them have distinct relation to the spirit of man. It is perfectly possible, and ultimately conceivable, that the crocodile and the lamb may have descended from the same ancestral atom of protoplasm; and that the physical laws of the operation of calcareous slime and of meadow grass, on that protoplasm, may in time have developed the opposite natures and aspects of the living frames; but the practically important fact for us is the existence of a power which creates that calcareous earth itself;—which creates, that separately—and quartz, separately; and gold, separately; and charcoal, separately; and then so directs the relation of these elements as that the gold shall destroy the souls of men by being yellow; and the charcoal destroy their souls by being hard and bright; and the quartz represent to them an ideal purity; and the calcareous earth, soft, shall beget crocodiles, and dry and hard, sheep; and

* The facts on which I am about to dwell are in nowise antagonistic to the theories which Mr. Darwin's unwearied and unerring investigations are every day rendering more probable. The æsthetic relations of species are independent of their origin. Nevertheless, it has always seemed to me, in what little work I have done upon organic forms, as if the species mocked us by their deliberate imitation of each other when they met: yet did not pass one into another.

that the aspects and qualities of these two products, crocodiles and lambs, shall be, the one repellent to the spirit of man, the other attractive to it, in a quite inevitable way; representing to him states of moral evil and good; and becoming myths to him of destruction or redemption, and, in the most literal sense, " words " of God.

63. And the force of these facts cannot be escaped from by the thought that there are species innumerable, passing into each other by regular gradations, out of which we choose what we most love or dread, and say they were indeed prepared for us. Species are not innumerable; neither are they now connected by consistent gradation. They touch at certain points only; and even then are connected, when we examine them deeply, in a kind of reticulated way, not in chains, but in chequers; also, however connected, it is but by a touch of the extremities, as it were, and the characteristic form of the species is entirely individual. The rose nearly sinks into a grass in the sanguisorba; but the formative spirit does not the less clearly separate the ear of wheat from the dog-rose, and oscillate with tremulous constancy round the central forms of both, having each their due relation to the mind of man. The great animal kingdoms are connected in the same way. The bird through the penguin drops towards the fish, and the fish in the cetacean reascends to the mammal, yet there is no confusion of thought possible between the perfect forms of an eagle, a trout, and a war-horse, in their relations to the elements, and to man.

64. Now we have two orders of animals to take some note of in connection with Athena, and one vast order of plants, which will illustrate this matter very sufficiently for us.

The orders of animals are the serpent and the bird; the serpent, in which the breath or spirit is less than in any other creature, and the earth-power greatest:—the bird, in which the breath or spirit is more full than in any other creature, and the earth power least.

65. We will take the bird first. It is little more than a drift of the air brought into form by plumes; the air is in all its quills, it breathes through its whole frame and flesh, and glows with air in its flying, like blown flame: it rests upon the air, subdues it, surpasses it, outraces it; —*is* the air, conscious of itself, conquering itself, ruling itself.

Also, into the throat of the bird is given the voice of the air. All that in the wind itself is weak, wild, useless in sweetness, is knit together in its song. As we may imagine the wild form of the cloud closed into the perfect form of the bird's wings, so the wild voice of the cloud into its ordered and commanded voice; unwearied, rippling through the clear heaven in its gladness, interpreting all intense passion through the soft spring nights, bursting into acclaim and rapture of choir at daybreak, or lisping and twittering among the boughs and hedges through heat of day, like little winds that only make the cowslip bells shake, and ruffle the petals of the wild rose.

66. Also, upon the plumes of the bird are put the colours of the air : on these the gold of the cloud, that cannot be gathered by any covetousness ; the rubies of the clouds, that are not the price of Athena, but *are* Athena ; the vermilion of the cloud-bar, and the flame of the cloud-crest, and the snow of the cloud, and its shadow, and the melted blue of the deep wells of the sky—all these, seized by the creating spirit, and woven by Athena herself into films and threads of plume ; with wave on wave following and fading along breast, and throat, and opened wings, infinite as the dividing of the foam and the sifting of the sea-sand ;—even the white down of the cloud seeming to flutter up between the stronger plumes, seen, but too soft for touch.

And so the Spirit of the Air is put into, and upon, this created form; and it becomes, through twenty centuries, the symbol of divine help, descending, as the Fire, to speak, but as the Dove, to bless.

67. Next, in the serpent, we approach the source of a group of myths, world-wide, founded on great and common human instincts, respecting which I must note one or two points which bear intimately on all our subject. For it seems to me that the scholars who are at present occupied in interpretation of human myths have most of them forgotten that there are any such things as natural myths; and that the dark sayings of men may be both difficult to read, and not always worth reading; but the dark sayings of nature will probably become clearer for

the looking into, and will very certainly be worth reading And, indeed, all guidance to the right sense of the human and variable myths will probably depend on our first getting at the sense of the natural and invariable ones. The dead hieroglyph may have meant this or that—the living hieroglyph means always the same; but remember, it is just as much a hieroglyph as the other; nay, more,— a "sacred or reserved sculpture," a thing with an inner language. The serpent crest of the king's crown, or of the god's, on the pillars of Egypt, is a mystery; but the serpent itself, gliding past the pillar's foot, is it less a mystery? Is there, indeed, no tongue, except the mute forked flash from its lips, in that running brook of horror on the ground?

68. Why that horror? We all feel it, yet how imaginative it is, how disproportioned to the real strength of the creature! There is more poison in an ill-kept drain,—in a pool of dish-washings at a cottage-door, than in the deadliest asp of Nile. Every back-yard which you look down into from the railway, as it carries you out by Vauxhall or Deptford, holds its coiled serpent: all the walls of those ghastly suburbs are enclosures of tank temples for serpent-worship; yet you feel no horror in looking down into them, as you would if you saw the livid scales, and lifted head. There is more venom, mortal, inevitable, in a single word, sometimes, or in the gliding entrance of a wordless thought, than ever "vanti Libia con sua rena." But that horror is of the myth, not

of the creature. There are myriads lower than this, and more loathsome, in the scale of being; the links between dead matter and animation drift everywhere unseen. But it is the strength of the base element that is so dreadful in the serpent; it is the very omnipotence of the earth. That rivulet of smooth silver—how does it flow, think you? It literally rows on the earth, with every scale for an oar; it bites the dust with the ridges of its body. Watch it, when it moves slowly:—A wave, but without wind! a current, but with no fall! all the body moving at the same instant, yet some of it to one side, some to another, or some forward, and the rest of the coil backwards; but all with the same calm will and equal way—no contraction, no extension; one soundless, causeless, march of sequent rings, and spectral procession of spotted dust, with dissolution in its fangs, dislocation in its coils. Startle it;—the winding stream will become a twisted arrow;—the wave of poisoned life will lash through the grass like a cast lance.* It scarcely breathes with its one lung (the other shrivelled and abortive); it is passive to the sun and shade, and is cold or hot like a

* I cannot understand this swift forward motion of serpents. The seizure of prey by the constrictor, though invisibly swift, is quite simple in mechanism; it is simply the return to its coil of an opened watch-spring, and is just as instantaneous. But the steady and continuous motion, without a visible fulcrum (for the whole body moves at the same instant, and I have often seen even small snakes glide as fast as I could walk), seems to involve a vibration of the scales quite too rapid to be conceived. The motion of the crest and dorsal fin of

stone; yet "it can outclimb the monkey, outswim the fish, outleap the zebra, outwrestle the athlete, and crush the tiger."* It is a divine hieroglyph of the demoniac power of the earth,—of the entire earthly nature. As the bird is the clothed power of the air, so this is the clothed power of the dust; as the bird the symbol of the spirit of life, so this of the grasp and sting of death.

69. Hence the continual change in the interpretation put upon it in various religions. As the worm of corruption, it is the mightiest of all adversaries of the gods—the special adversary of their light and creative power—Python against Apollo. As the power of the earth against the air, the giants are serpent-bodied in the Giganto-machia; but as the power of the earth upon the seed—consuming it into new life ("that which thou sowest is not quickened except it die")—serpents sustain the chariot of the spirit of agriculture.

70. Yet, on the other hand, there is a power in the earth to take away corruption, and to purify, (hence the very fact of burial, and many uses of earth, only lately known); and in this sense, the serpent is a healing

the hippocampus, which is one of the intermediate types between serpent and fish, perhaps gives some resemblance of it, dimly visible, for the quivering turns the fin into a mere mist. The entrance of the two barbs of a bee's sting by alternate motion, "the teeth of one barb acting as a fulcrum for the other," must be something like the serpent motion on a small scale.

* Richard Owen.

spirit,—the representative of Æsculapius, and of Hygieia; and is a sacred earth-type in the temple of the Dew;— being there especially a symbol of the native earth of Athens; so that its departure from the temple was a sign to the Athenians that they were to leave their homes. And then, lastly, as there is a strength and healing in the earth, no less than the strength of air, so there is conceived to be a wisdom of earth no less than a wisdom of the spirit; and when its deadly power is killed, its guiding power becomes true; so that the Python serpent is killed at Delphi, where yet the oracle is from the breath of the earth.

71. You must remember, however, that in this, as in every other instance, I take the myth at its central time. This is only the meaning of the serpent to the Greek mind which could conceive an Athena. Its first meaning to the nascent eyes of men, and its continued influence over degraded races, are subjects of the most fearful mystery. Mr. Fergusson has just collected the principal evidence bearing on the matter in a work of very great value, and if you read his opening chapters, they will put you in possession of the circumstances needing chiefly to be considered. I cannot touch upon any of them here, except only to point out that, though the doctrine of the so-called "corruption of human nature," asserting that there is nothing but evil in humanity, is just as blasphemous and false as a doctrine of the corruption of physical nature would be, asserting there was nothing but evil in the

earth,—there is yet the clearest evidence of a disease, plague, or cretinous imperfection of development, hitherto allowed to prevail against the greater part of the races of men; and this in monstrous ways, more full of mystery than the serpent-being itself. I have gathered for you tonight only instances of what is beautiful in Greek religion; but even in its best time there were deep corruptions in other phases of it, and degraded forms of many of its deities, all originating in a misunderstood worship of the principle of life; while in the religions of lower races, little else than these corrupted forms of devotion can be found;—all having a strange and dreadful consistency with each other, and infecting Christianity, even at its strongest periods, with fatal terror of doctrine, and ghastliness of symbolic conception, passing through fear into frenzied grotesque, and thence into sensuality.

In the Psalter of St. Louis itself, half of its letters are twisted snakes; there is scarcely a wreathed ornament, employed in Christian dress, or architecture, which cannot be traced back to the serpent's coil; and there is rarely a piece of monkish decorated writing in the world, that is not tainted with some ill-meant vileness of grotesque— nay, the very leaves of the twisted ivy-pattern of the fourteenth century can be followed back to wreaths for the foreheads of bacchanalian gods. And truly, it seems to me, as I gather in my mind the evidences of insane religion, degraded art, merciless war, sullen toil, detestable pleasure, and vain or vile hope, in which the nations of the world have lived since first they could bear record of themselves—it seems to me, I say, as if the race itself were still half-serpent, not extricated yet from its clay; a lacertine breed of bitterness—the glory of it emaciate with cruel hunger, and blotted with venomous stain: and the track of it, on the leaf a glittering slime, and in the sand a useless furrow.

72. There are no myths, therefore, by which the moral state and fineness of intelligence of different races can be so deeply tried or measured, as by those of the serpent and the bird; both of them having an especial relation to the kind of remorse for sin, or grief in fate, of which the national minds that spoke by them had been capable. The serpent and vulture are alike emblems of immortality and purification among races which desired to be immortal and pure: and as they recognize their own misery, the serpent becomes to them the scourge of the Furies, and the vulture finds its eternal prey in their breast. The bird long contests among the Egyptians with the still received serpent symbol of power. But the Draconian image of evil is established in the serpent Apap; while the bird's wings, with the globe, become part of a better symbol of deity, and the entire form of the vulture, as an emblem of purification, is associated with the earliest conception of Athena. In the type of the dove with the olive branch, the conception of the spirit of Athena in renewed life prevailing over ruin, is embodied for the whole of futurity; while the Greeks, to whom, in a hap-

pier climate and higher life than that of Egypt, the vulture symbol of cleansing became unintelligible, took the eagle, instead, for their hieroglyph of supreme spiritual energy, and it thenceforward retains its hold on the human imagination, till it is established among Christian myths as the expression of the most exalted form of evangelistic teaching. The special relation of Athena to her favourite bird we will trace presently: the peacock of Hera, and dove of Aphrodite, are comparatively unimportant myths: but the bird power is soon made entirely human by the Greeks in their flying angel of victory (partially human, with modified meaning of evil, in the Harpy and Siren); and thenceforward it associates itself with the Hebrew cherubim, and has had the most singular influence on the Christian religion by giving its wings to render the conception of angels mysterious and untenable, and check rational endeavour to determine the nature of subordinate spiritual agency; while yet it has given to that agency a vague poetical influence of the highest value in its own imaginative way.

73. But with the early serpent worship there was associated another—that of the groves—of which you will also find the evidence exhaustively collected in Mr. Fergusson's work. This tree-worship may have taken a dark form when associated with the Draconian one; or opposed, as in Judea, to a purer faith; but in itself, I believe, it was always healthy, and though it retains little definite hieroglyphic power in subsequent religion, it becomes,

instead of symbolic, real; the flowers and trees are themselves beheld and beloved with a half-worshipping delight, which is always noble and healthful.

And it is among the most notable indications of the volition of the animating power, that we find the ethical signs of good and evil set on these also, as well as upon animals; the venom of the serpent, and in some respects its image also, being associated even with the passionless growth of the leaf out of the ground; while the distinctions of species seem appointed with more definite ethical address to the intelligence of man as their material products become more useful to him.

74. I can easily show this, and, at the same time, make clear the relation to other plants of the flowers which especially belong to Athena, by examining the natural myths in the groups of the plants which would be used at any country dinner, over which Athena would, in her simplest household authority, cheerfully rule, here, in England. Suppose Horace's favourite dish of beans, with the bacon; potatoes; some savoury stuffing of onions and herbs with the meat; celery, and a radish or two, with the cheese; nuts and apples for dessert, and brown bread.

75. The beans are, from earliest time, the most important and interesting of the seeds of the great tribe of plants from which came the Latin and French name for all kitchen vegetables,—things that are gathered with the hand—podded seeds that cannot be reaped, or beaten, or shaken down, but must be gathered green. "Legumi-

nous" plants, all of them having flowers like butterflies, seeds in (frequently pendent) pods,—"lætum siliqua quassante legumen"—smooth and tender leaves, divided into many minor ones;—strange adjuncts of tendril, for climbing (and sometimes of thorn);—exquisitely sweet, yet pure, scents of blossom, and almost always harmless, if not serviceable, seeds. It is, of all tribes of plants, the most definite; its blossoms being entirely limited in their parts, and not passing into other forms. It is also the most usefully extended in range and scale; familiar in the height of the forest—acacia, laburnum, Judas-tree; familiar in the sown field—bean and vetch and pea; familiar in the pasture—in every form of clustered clover and sweet trefoil tracery; the most entirely serviceable and human of all orders of plants.

76. Next, in the potato, we have the scarcely innocent underground stem of one of a tribe set aside for evil; having the deadly nightshade for its queen, and including the henbane, the witch's mandrake, and the worst natural curse of modern civilization—tobacco.* And the strange thing about this tribe is, that though thus set aside for evil, they are not a group distinctly separate from those that are happier in function. There is nothing in other tribes of plants like the form of the bean blossom; but there is another family with forms and structure closely connected

* It is not easy to estimate the demoralizing effect on the youth of Europe of the cigar, in enabling them to pass their time happily in idleness.

with this venomous one. Examine the purple and yellow bloom of the common hedge nightshade; you will find it constructed exactly like some of the forms of the cyclamen; and, getting this clue, you will find at last the whole poisonous and terrible group to be—sisters of the primulas!

The nightshades are, in fact, primroses with a curse upon them; and a sign set in their petals, by which the deadly and condemned flowers may always be known from the innocent ones,—that the stamens of the nightshades are between the lobes, and of the primulas, opposite the lobes, of the corolla.

77. Next, side by side, in the celery and radish, you have the two great groups of umbelled and cruciferous plants; alike in conditions of rank among herbs: both flowering in clusters; but the umbelled group, flat, the crucifers, in spires:—both of them mean and poor in the blossom, and losing what beauty they have by too close crowding:—both of them having the most curious influence on human character in the temperate zones of the earth, from the days of the parsley crown, and hemlock drink, and mocked Euripidean chervil, until now: but chiefly among the northern nations, being especially plants that are of some humble beauty, and (the crucifers) of endless use, when they are chosen and cultivated; but that run to wild waste, and are the signs of neglected ground, in their rank or ragged leaves, and meagre stalks, and pursed or podded seed clusters. Capable, even under cultivation,

of no perfect beauty, though reaching some subdued delightfulness in the lady's smock and the wallflower; for the most part, they have every floral quality meanly, and in vain,—they are white, without purity; golden, without preciousness; redundant, without richness; divided, without fineness; massive, without strength; and slender, without grace. Yet think over that useful vulgarity of theirs; and of the relations of German and English peasant character to its food of kraut and cabbage, (as of Arab character to its food of palm-fruit,) and you will begin to feel what purposes of the forming spirit are in these distinctions of species.

78. Next we take the nuts and apples,—the nuts representing one of the groups of catkined trees, whose blossoms are only tufts and dust; and the other, the rose tribe, in which fruit and flower alike have been the types, to the highest races of men, of all passionate temptation, or pure delight, from the coveting of Eve to the crowning of the Madonna, above the

> "Rosa sempiterna,
> Che si dilata, rigrada, e ridole
> Odor di lode al Sol."

We have no time now for these, we must go on to the humblest group of all, yet the most wonderful, that of the grass, which has given us our bread; and from that we will go back to the herbs.

79. The vast family of plants which, under rain, make the earth green for man, and, under sunshine, give him

bread, and, in their springing in the early year, mixed with their native flowers, have given us (far more than the new leaves of trees) the thought and word of "spring," divide themselves broadly into three great groups—the grasses, sedges, and rushes. The grasses are essentially a clothing for healthy and pure ground, watered by occasional rain, but in itself dry, and fit for all cultivated pasture and corn. They are distinctively plants with round and jointed stems, which have long green flexible leaves, and heads of seed, independently emerging from them. The sedges are essentially the clothing of waste and more or less poor or uncultivable soils, coarse in their structure, frequently triangular in stem—hence called "acute" by Virgil—and with their heads of seed not extricated from their leaves. Now, in both the sedges and grasses, the blossom has a common structure, though undeveloped in the sedges, but composed always of groups of double husks, which have mostly a spinous process in the centre, sometimes projecting into a long awn or beard; this central process being characteristic also of the ordinary leaves of mosses, as if a moss were a kind of ear of corn made permanently green on the ground, and with a new and distinct fructification. But the rushes differ wholly from the sedge and grass in their blossom structure. It is not a dual cluster, but a twice threefold one, so far separate from the grasses, and so closely connected with a higher order of plants, that I think you will find it convenient to group the rushes at once with that higher order, to which, if you will for the present let me give the general name of Drosidæ, or dew-plants, it will enable me to say what I have to say of them much more shortly and clearly.

80. These Drosidæ, then, are plants delighting in interrupted moisture—moisture which comes either partially or at certain seasons—into dry ground. They are not water-plants; but the signs of water resting among dry places. Many of the true water-plants have triple blossoms, with a small triple calyx holding them; in the Drosidæ, the floral spirit passes into the calyx also, and the entire flower becomes a six-rayed star, bursting out of the stem laterally, as if it were the first of flowers, and had made its way to the light by force through the unwilling green. They are often required to retain moisture or nourishment for the future blossom through long times of drought; and this they do in bulbs under ground, of which some become a rude and simple, but most wholesome, food for man.

81. So now, observe, you are to divide the whole family of the herbs of the field into three great groups—Drosidæ, Carices,* Gramineæ—dew-plants, sedges, and grasses. Then, the Drosidæ are divided into five great orders—lilies, asphodels, amaryllids, irids, and rushes. No tribes of flowers have had so great, so varied, or so healthy an influence on man as this great group of Drosidæ, depending,

* I think Carex will be found ultimately better than Cyperus for the generic name, being the Virgilian word, and representing a larger sub-species.

not so much on the whiteness of some of their blossoms, or the radiance of others, as on the strength and delicacy of the substance of their petals; enabling them to take forms of faultless elastic curvature, either in cups, as the crocus, or expanding bells, as the true lily, or heath-like bells, as the hyacinth, or bright and perfect stars, like the star of Bethlehem, or, when they are affected by the strange reflex of the serpent nature which forms the labiate group of all flowers, closing into forms of exquisitely fantastic symmetry in the gladiolus. Put by their side their Nereid sisters, the water-lilies, and you have in them the origin of the loveliest forms of ornamental design, and the most powerful floral myths yet recognized among human spirits, born by the streams of Ganges, Nile, Arno, and Avon.

82. For consider a little what each of those five tribes* has been to the spirit of man. First, in their nobleness : the Lilies gave the lily of the Annunciation ; the Asphodels, the flower of the Elysian fields ; the Irids, the fleur-de-lys of chivalry ; and the Amaryllids, Christ's lily of the field : while the rush, trodden always under foot, became the emblem of humility. Then take each of the tribes, and consider the extent of their lower influence. Perdita's

* Take this rough distinction of the four tribes :—Lilies, superior ovary, white seeds ; Asphodels, superior ovary, black seeds ; Irids, inferior ovary, style (typically) rising into central crest ; Amaryllids, inferior ovary, stamens (typically) joined in central cup. Then tho rushes are a dark group, through which they stoop to the grasses.

"The crown imperial, lilies of all kinds," are the first tribe; which, giving the type of perfect purity in the Madonna's lily, have, by their lovely form, influenced the entire decorative design of Italian sacred art; while ornament of war was continually enriched by the curves of the triple petals of the Florentine "giglio," and French fleur-de-lys; so that it is impossible to count their influence for good in the middle ages, partly as a symbol of womanly character, and partly of the utmost brightness and refinement of chivalry in the city which was the flower of cities.

Afterwards, the group of the turban-lilies, or tulips, did some mischief, (their splendid stains having made them the favourite caprice of florists;) but they may be pardoned all such guilt for the pleasure they have given in cottage gardens, and are yet to give, when lowly life may again be possible among us; and the crimson bars of the tulips in their trim beds, with their likeness in crimson bars of morning above them, and its dew glittering heavy, globed in their glossy cups, may be loved better than the gray nettles of the ash heap, under gray sky, unveined by vermilion or by gold.

83. The next great group, of the Asphodels, divides itself also into two principal families; one, in which the flowers are like stars, and clustered characteristically in balls, though opening sometimes into looser heads; and the other, in which the flowers are in long bells, opening suddenly at the lips, and clustered in spires on a long stem, or drooping from it, when bent by their weight.

The star-group, of the squills, garlics, and onions, has always caused me great wonder. I cannot understand why its beauty, and serviceableness, should have been associated with the rank scent which has been really among the most powerful means of degrading peasant life, and separating it from that of the higher classes.

The belled group, of the hyacinth and convallaria, is as delicate as the other is coarse: the unspeakable azure light along the ground of the wood hyacinth in English spring; the grape hyacinth, which is in south France, as if a cluster of grapes and a hive of honey had been distilled and compressed together into one small boss of celled and beaded blue; the lilies of the valley everywhere, in each sweet and wild recess of rocky lands;—count the influences of these on childish and innocent life; then measure the mythic power of the hyacinth and asphodel as connected with Greek thoughts of immortality; finally take their useful and nourishing power in ancient and modern peasant life, and it will be strange if you do not feel what fixed relation exists between the agency of the creating spirit in these, and in us who live by them.

84. It is impossible to bring into any tenable compass for our present purpose, even hints of the human influence of the two remaining orders of Amaryllids and Irids;—only note this generally, that while these in northern countries share with the Primulas the fields of spring, it seems that in Greece, the primulaceæ are not an extended tribe, while the crocus, narcissus, and Amaryllis

lutea, the "lily of the field" (I suspect also that the flower whose name we translate "violet" was in truth an Iris) represented to the Greek the first coming of the breath of life on the renewed herbage; and became in his thoughts the true embroidery of the saffron robe of Athena. Later in the year, the dianthus (which, though belonging to an entirely different race of plants, has yet a strange look of having been made out of the grasses by turning the sheath-membrane at the root of their leaves into a flower,) seems to scatter, in multitudinous families, its crimson stars far and wide. But the golden lily and crocus, together with the asphodel, retain always the old Greek's fondest thoughts—they are only "golden" flowers that are to burn on the trees, and float on the streams of paradise.

85. I have but one tribe of plants more to note at our country feast—the savoury herbs; but must go a little out of my way to come at them rightly. All flowers whose petals are fastened together, and most of those whose petals are loose, are best thought of first as a kind of cup or tube opening at the mouth. Sometimes the opening is gradual, as in the convolvulus or campanula; oftener there is a distinct change of direction between the tube and expanding lip, as in the primrose; or even a contraction under the lip, making the tube into a narrow-necked phial or vase, as in the heaths, but the general idea of a tube expanding into a quatrefoil, cinquefoil, or sixfoil, will embrace most of the forms.

86. Now it is easy to conceive that flowers of this kind, growing in close clusters, may, in process of time, have extended their outside petals rather than the interior ones (as the outer flowers of the clusters of many umbellifers actually do), and thus; elongated and variously distorted forms have established themselves; then if the stalk is attached to the side instead of the base of the tube, its base becomes a spur, and thus all the grotesque forms of the mints, violets, and larkspurs, gradually might be composed. But, however this may be, there is one great tribe of plants separate from the rest, and of which the influence seems shed upon the rest in different degrees: and these would give the impression, not so much of having been developed by change, as of being stamped with a character of their own, more or less serpentine or dragon-like. And I think you will find it convenient to call these generally, *Draconidæ;* disregarding their present ugly botanical name, which I do not care even to write once—you may take for their principal types the Foxglove, Snapdragon, and Calceolaria; and you will find they all agree in a tendency to decorate themselves by spots, and with bosses or swollen places in their leaves, as if they had been touched by poison. The spot of the Foxglove is especially strange, because it draws the colour out of the tissue all around it, as if it had been stung, and as if the central colour was really an inflamed spot, with paleness round. Then also they carry to its extreme the deco-

ration by bulging or pouting the petal;—often beautifully used by other flowers in a minor degree, like the beating out of bosses in hollow silver, as in the kalmia, beaten out apparently in each petal by the stamens instead of a hammer; or the borage, pouting inwards; but the snapdragons and calceolarias carry it to its extreme.

87. Then the spirit of these Draconidæ seems to pass more or less into other flowers, whose forms are properly pure vases; but it affects some of them slightly,—others not at all. It never strongly affects the heaths; never once the roses; but it enters like an evil spirit into the buttercup, and turns it into a larkspur, with a black, spotted, grotesque centre, and a strange, broken blue, gorgeous and intense, yet impure, glittering on the surface as if it were strewn with broken glass, and stained or darkening irregularly into red. And then at last the serpent charm changes the ranunculus into monkshood; and makes it poisonous. It enters into the forget-me-not, and the star of heavenly turquoise is corrupted into the viper's bugloss, darkened with the same strange red as the larkspur, and fretted into a fringe of thorn; it enters, together with a strange insect-spirit, into the asphodels, and (though with a greater interval between the groups,) they change into spotted orchideæ: it touches the poppy, it becomes a fumaria; the iris, and it pouts into a gladiolus; the lily, and it chequers itself into a snake's-head, and secretes in the deep of its bell, drops, not of venom indeed, but honey-dew, as if it were a healing serpent.

For there is an Æsculapian as well as an evil serpentry among the Draconidæ, and the fairest of them, the "erba della Madonna" of Venice, (Linaria Cymbalaria,) descends from the ruins it delights in to the herbage at their feet, and touches it; and behold, instantly, a vast group of herbs for healing,—all draconid in form,—spotted, and crested, and from their lip-like corollas named "labiatæ;" full of various balm, and warm strength for healing, yet all of them without splendid honour or perfect beauty, "ground ivies," richest when crushed under the foot; the best sweetness and gentle brightness of the robes of the field,—thyme, and marjoram, and Euphrasy.

88. And observe, again and again, with respect to all these divisions and powers of plants; it does not matter in the least by what concurrences of circumstance or necessity they may gradually have been developed: the concurrence of circumstance is itself the supreme and inexplicable fact. We always come at last to a formative cause, which directs the circumstance, and mode of meeting it. If you ask an ordinary botanist the reason of the form of a leaf, he will tell you it is a "developed tubercle," and that its ultimate form "is owing to the directions of its vascular threads." But what directs its vascular threads? "They are seeking for something they want," he will probably answer. What made them want that? What made them seek for it thus? Seek for it, in five fibres or in three? Seek for it, in serration, or in

sweeping curves? Seek for it, in servile tendrils, or impetuous spray? Seek for it, in woollen wrinkles rough with stings, or in glossy surfaces,-green with pure strength, and winterless delight?

89. There is no answer. But the sum of all is, that over the entire surface of the earth and its waters, as influenced by the power of the air under solar light, there is developed a series of changing forms, in clouds, plants, and animals, all of which have reference in their action, or nature, to the human intelligence that perceives them; and on which, in their aspects of horror and beauty, and their qualities of good and evil, there is engraved a series of myths, or words of the forming power, which, according to the true passion and energy of the human race, they have been enabled to read into religion. And this forming power has been by all nations partly confused with the breath or air through which it acts, and partly understood as a creative wisdom, proceeding from the Supreme Deity; but entering into and inspiring all intelligences that work in harmony with Him. And whatever intellectual results may be in modern days obtained by regarding this effluence only as a motion of vibration, every formative human art hitherto, and the best states of human happiness and order, have depended on the apprehension of its mystery (which is certain), and of its personality, which is probable.

90. Of its influence on the formative arts, I have a few words to say separately: my present business is only to

interpret, as we are now sufficiently enabled to do, the external symbols of the myth under which it was represented by the Greeks as a goddess of counsel, taken first into the breast of their supreme Deity, then created out of his thoughts, and abiding closely beside him; always sharing and consummating his power.

91. And in doing this we have first to note the meaning of the principal epithet applied to Athena, " Glaukopis," " with eyes full of light," the first syllable being connected, by its root, with words signifying sight, not with words signifying colour. As far as I can trace the colour perception of the Greeks, I find it all founded primarily on the degree of connection between colour and light; the most important fact to them in the colour of red being its connection with fire and sunshine; so that " purple " is, in its original sense, " fire-colour," and the scarlet, or orange, of dawn, more than any other fire-colour. I was long puzzled by Homer's calling the sea purple; and misled into thinking he meant the colour of cloud shadows on green sea; whereas he really means the gleaming blaze of the waves under wide light. Aristotle's idea (partly true) is that light, subdued by blackness, becomes red; and blackness, heated or lighted, also becomes red. Thus, a colour may be called purple because it is light subdued (and so death is called " purple " or " shadowy " death); or else it may be called purple as being shade kindled with fire, and thus said of the lighted sea; or even of the sun itself, when it is thought

of as a red luminary opposed to the whiteness of the moon: "purpureos inter soles, et candida lunæ sidera;" or of golden hair: "pro purpureo poenam solvens sceletata capillo;" while both ideas are modified by the influence of an earlier form of the word, which has nothing to do with fire at all, but only with mixing or staining; and then, to make the whole group of thoughts inextricably complex, yet rich and subtle in proportion to their intricacy, the various rose and crimson colours of the murex-dye,—the crimson and purple of the poppy, and fruit of the palm,—and the association of all these with the hue of blood;—partly direct, partly through a confusion between the word signifying "slaughter" and "palm-fruit colour," mingle themselves in, and renew the whole nature of the old word; so that, in later literature, it means a different colour, or emotion of colour, in almost every place where it occurs; and casts forever around the reflection of all that has been dipped in its dyes.

92. So that the word is really a liquid prism, and stream of opal. And then, last of all, to keep the whole history of it in the fantastic course of a dream, warped here and there into wild grotesque, we moderns, who have preferred to rule over coal-mines instead of the sea (and so have turned the everlasting lamp of Athena into a Davy's safety-lamp in the hand of Britannia, and Athenian heavenly lightning into British subterranean "damp"), have actually got our purple out of coal instead of the sea! And thus, grotesquely, we have had enforced

on us the doubt that held the old word between blackness and fire, and have completed the shadow, and the fear of it, by giving it a name from battle, "Magenta."

93. There is precisely a similar confusion between light and colour in the word used for the blue of the eyes of Athena—a noble confusion, however, brought about by the intensity of the Greek sense that the heaven is light, more than that it is blue. I was not thinking of this when I wrote, in speaking of pictorial chiaroscuro, " The sky is not blue colour merely : it is blue fire, and cannot be painted" (Mod. P. iv. p. 36); but it was this that the Greeks chiefly felt of it, and so " Glaukopis" chiefly means gray-eyed : gray standing for a pale or luminous blue; but it only means, " owl-eyed " in thought of the roundness and expansion, not from the colour; this breadth and brightness being, again, in their moral sense typical cf the breadth, intensity, and singleness of the sight in prudence (" if thine eye be single, thy whole body shall be full of light "). Then the actual power of the bird to see in twilight enters into the type, and perhaps its general fineness of sense. " Before the human form was adopted, her (Athena's) proper symbol was the owl, a bird which seems to surpass all other creatures in acuteness of organic perception, its eye being calculated to observe objects which to all others are enveloped in darkness, its ear to hear sounds distinctly, and its nostrils to discriminate effluvia with such nicety that it has been deemed prophetic,

from discovering the putridity of death even in the first stages of disease."*

I cannot find anywhere an account of the first known occurrence of the type; but, in the early ones on Attic coins, the wide round eyes are clearly the principal things to be made manifest.

94. There is yet, however, another colour of great importance in the conception of Athena—the dark blue of her ægis. Just as the blue or gray of her eyes was conceived as more light than colour, so her ægis was dark blue, because the Greeks thought of this tint more as shade than colour, and, while they used various materials in ornamentation, lapislazuli, carbonate of copper, or perhaps, smalt, with real enjoyment of the blue tint, it was yet in their minds as distinctly representative of darkness as scarlet was of light, and, therefore, anything dark,† but

---

* Payne Knight in his "Inquiry into the Symbolical Language of Ancient Art," not trustworthy, being little more than a mass of conjectural memoranda, but the heap is suggestive, if well sifted.

† In the breastplate and shield of Atrides the serpents and bosses are all of this dark colour, yet the serpents are said to be like rainbows; but through all this splendour and opposition of hue, I feel distinctly that the literal "splendour," with its relative shade, are prevalent in the conception; and that there is always a tendency to look through the hue to its cause. And in this feeling about colour the Greeks are separated from the eastern nations, and from the best designers of Christian times. I cannot find that they take pleasure in colour for its own sake; it may be in something more than colour, or better; but it is not in the hue itself. When Homer describes cloud breaking from a mountain summit, the crags became visible in light, not in colour; he

especially the colour of heavy thunder-cloud, was described by the same term. The physical power of this darkness of the ægis, fringed with lightning, is given quite simply when Jupiter himself uses it to overshadow Ida and the Plain of Troy, and withdraws it at the prayer of Ajax for light; and again when he grants it to be worn

feels only their flashing out in bright edges and trenchant shadows : above, the "infinite," "unspeakable" æther is torn open—but not the *blue* of it. He has scarcely any abstract pleasure in blue, or green, or gold ; but only in their shade or flame.

I have yet to trace the causes of this (which will be a long task, belonging to art questions, not to mythological ones); but it is, I believe, much connected with the brooding of the shadow of death over the Greeks without any clear hope of immortality. The restriction of the colour on their vases to dim red (or yellow) with black and white, is greatly connected with their sepulchral use, and with all the melancholy of Greek tragic thought ; and in this gloom the failure of colour-perception is partly noble, partly base : noble, in its earnestness, which raises the design of Greek vases as far above the designing of mere colourist nations like the Chinese, as men's thoughts are above children's ; and yet it is partly base and earthly; and inherently defective in one human faculty : and I believe it was one cause of the perishing of their art so swiftly, for indeed there is no decline so sudden, or down to such utter loss and ludicrous depravity, as the fall of Greek design on its vases from the fifth to the third century, B.C. On the other hand, the pure coloured-gift, when employed for pleasure only, degrades in another direction ; so that among the Indians, Chinese, and Japanese, all intellectual progress in art has been for ages rendered impossible by the prevalence of that faculty : and yet it is, as I have said again and again, the spiritual power of art; and its true brightness is the essential characteristic of all healthy schools.

for a time by Apollo, who is hidden by its cloud when he
strikes down Patroclus: but its spiritual power is chiefly
expressed by a word signifying deeper shadow ;—the gloom
of Erebus, or of our evening, which, when spoken of the
ægis, signifies, not merely the indignation of Athena, but
the entire hiding or withdrawal of her help, and beyond
even this, her deadliest of all hostility,—the darkness by
which she herself deceives and beguiles to final ruin those
to whom she is wholly adverse; this contradiction of her
own glory being the uttermost judgment upon human
falsehood. Thus it is she who provokes Pandarus to the
treachery which purposed to fulfil the rape of Helen by
the murder of her husband in time of truce; and *then* the
Greek King, holding his wounded brother's hand, prophesies against Troy the darkness of the ægis which shall be
over all, and for ever. *

95. This, then, finally, was the perfect colour-conception
of Athena;—the flesh, snow-white, (the hands, feet, and
face of marble, even when the statue was hewn roughly in
wood); the eyes of keen pale blue, often in statues represented by jewels; the long robe to the feet, crocus-coloured;
and the ægis thrown over it of thunderous purple; the
helmet golden, (Il. v. 744), and I suppose its crest also, as
that of Achilles.

If you think carefully of the meaning and character
which is now enough illustrated for you in each of these
colours; and remember that the crocus-colour and the pur-

---

* ἐρεμνὴν Αἰγίδα πᾶσι.—Il. iv. 166.

ple were both of them developments, in opposite directions, of the great central idea of fire-colour, or scarlet, you will see that this form of the creative spirit of the earth is conceived as robed in the blue, and purple, and scarlet, the white, and the gold, which have been recognized for the sacred chord of colours, from the day when the cloud descended on a Rock more mighty than Ida.

96. I have spoken throughout, hitherto, of the conception of Athena, as it is traceable in the Greek mind; not as it was rendered by Greek art. It is matter of extreme difficulty, requiring a sympathy at once affectionate and cautious, and a knowledge reaching the earliest springs of the religion of many lands, to discern through the imperfection, and, alas! more dimly yet, through the triumphs, of formative art, what kind of thoughts they were that appointed for it the tasks of its childhood, and watched by the awakening of its strength.

The religious passion is nearly always vividest when the art is weakest; and the technical skill only reaches its deliberate splendour when the ecstasy which gave it birth has passed away for ever. It is as vain an attempt to reason out the visionary power or guiding influence of Athena in the Greek heart, from anything we now read, or possess, of the work of Phidias, as it would be for the disciples of some new religion to infer the spirit of Christianity from Titian's "Assumption." The effective vitality of the religious conception can be traced only through the efforts of trembling hands, and strange pleasures of untaught eyes; and the beauty of the dream can no more be found in the first symbols by which it is expressed, than a child's idea of fairyland can be gathered from its pencil scrawl, or a girl's love for her broken doll explained by the defaced features. On the other hand, the Athena of Phidias was, in very fact, not so much the deity, as the darling of the Athenian people. Her magnificence represented their pride and fondness, more than their piety; and the great artist, in lavishing upon her dignities which might be ended abruptly by the pillage they provoked, resigned, apparently without regret, the awe of her ancient memory; and (with only the careless remonstrance of a workman too strong to be proud,) even the perfectness of his own art. Rejoicing in the protection of their goddess, and in their own hour of glory, the people of Athena robed her, at their will, with the preciousness of ivory and gems; forgot or denied the darkness of the breastplate of judgment, and vainly bade its unappeasable serpents relax their coils in gold.

97. It will take me many a day yet—if days, many or few, are given me—to disentangle in anywise the proud and practised disguises of religious creeds from the instinctive arts which, grotesquely and indecorously, yet with sincerity, strove to embody them, or to relate. But I think the reader, by help even of the imperfect indications already given to him, will be able to follow, with a continually increasing security, the vestiges of the Myth of Athena; and to reanimate its almost evanescent shade,

by connecting it with the now recognized facts of existent nature, which it, more or less dimly, reflected and foretold. I gather these facts together in brief sum.

98. The deep of air that surrounds the earth enters into union with the earth at its surface, and with its waters; so as to be the apparent cause of their ascending into life. First, it warms them, and shades, at once, staying the heat of the sun's rays in its own body, but warding their force with its clouds. It warms and cools at once, with traffic of balm and frost; so that the white wreaths are withdrawn from the field of the Swiss peasant by the glow of Libyan rock. It gives its own strength to the sea; forms and fills every cell of its foam; sustains the precipices, and designs the valleys of its waves; gives the gleam to their moving under the night, and the white fire to their plains under sunrise; lifts their voices along the rocks, bears above them the spray of birds, pencils through them the dimpling of unfooted sands. It gathers out of them a portion in the hollow of its hand: dyes, with that, the hills into dark blue, and their glaciers with dying rose; inlays with that, for sapphire, the dome in which it has to set the cloud; shapes out of that the heavenly flocks: divides them, numbers, cherishes, bears them on its bosom, calls them to their journeys, waits by their rest; feeds from them the brooks that cease not, and strews with them the dews that cease. It spins and weaves their fleece into wild tapestry, rends it, and renews; and flits and flames, and whispers, among the golden threads,

thrilling them with a plectrum of strange fire that traverses them to and fro, and is enclosed in them like life.

It enters into the surface of the earth, subdues it, and falls together with it into fruitful dust, from which can be moulded flesh; it joins itself, in dew, to the substance of adamant; and becomes the green leaf out of the dry ground; it enters into the separated shapes of the earth it has tempered, commands the ebb and flow of the current of their life, fills their limbs with its own lightness, measures their existence by its indwelling pulse, moulds upon their lips the words by which one soul can be known to another; is to them the hearing of the ear, and the beating of the heart; and, passing away, leaves them to the peace that hears and moves no more.

99. This was the Athena of the greatest people of the days of old. And opposite to the temple of this Spirit of the breath, and life-blood, of man and of beast, stood, on the Mount of Justice, and near the chasm which was haunted by the goddess-Avengers, an altar to a God unknown;—proclaimed at last to them, as one who, indeed, gave to all men, life, and breath, and all things; and rain from heaven, filling their hearts with food and gladness; —a God who had made of one blood all nations of men who dwell on the face of all the earth, and had determined the times of their fate, and the bounds of their habitation.

100. We ourselves, fretted here in our narrow days, know less, perhaps, in very deed, than they, what manner of spirit we are of, or what manner of spirit we ignorantly

worship. Have we, indeed, desired the Desire of all nations? and will the Master whom we meant to seek, and the Messenger in whom we thought we delighted, confirm, when He comes to His temple,—or not find in its midst, —the tables heavy with gold for bread, and the seats that are bought with the price of the dove? Or is our own land also to be left by its angered Spirit;—left among those, where sunshine vainly sweet, and passionate folly of storm, waste themselves in the silent places of knowledge that has passed away, and of tongues that have ceased?

This only we may discern assuredly: this, every true light of science, every mercifully-granted power, every wisely-restricted thought, teach us more clearly day by day, that in the heavens above, and the earth beneath, there is one continual and omnipotent presence of help, and of peace, for all men who know that they Live, and remember that they Die.

III.

ATHENA ERGANE.*

(*Athena in the Heart.*)

Various Notes relating to the Conception of Athena as the Directress of the Imagination and Will.

101. I HAVE now only a few words to say, bearing on what seems to me present need, respecting the third function of Athena, conceived as the directress of human passion, resolution, and labour.

Few words, for I am not yet prepared to give accurate distinction between the intellectual rule of Athena and that of the Muses: but, broadly, the Muses, with their king, preside over meditative, historical, and poetic arts, whose end is the discovery of light or truth, and the creation of beauty: but Athena rules over moral passion, and practically useful art. She does not make men learned, but prudent and subtle: she does not teach them to make their work beautiful, but to make it right.

In different places of my writings, and through many years of endeavour to define the laws of art, I have insisted on this rightness in work, and on its connection

---

* "Athena the worker, or having rule over work." The name was first given to her by the Athenians.

with virtue of character, in so many partial ways, that the impression left on the reader's mind—if, indeed, it was ever impressed at all—has been confused and uncertain. In beginning the series of my corrected works, I wish this principle (in my own mind the foundation of every other) to be made plain, if nothing else is: and will try, therefore, to make it so, as far as, by any effort, I can put it into unmistakeable words. And, first, here is a very simple statement of it, given lately in a lecture on the Architecture of the Valley of the Somme, which will be better read in this place than in its incidental connection with my account of the porches of Abbeville.

102. I had used, in a preceding part of the lecture, the expression, "by what faults" this Gothic architecture fell. We continually speak thus of works of art. We talk of their faults and merits, as of virtues and vices. What do we mean by talking of the faults of a picture, or the merits of a piece of stone?

The faults of a work of art are the faults of its workman, and its virtues his virtues.

Great art is the expression of the mind of a great man, and mean art, that of the want of mind of a weak man. A foolish person builds foolishly, and a wise one, sensibly; a virtuous one, beautifully; and a vicious one, basely. If stone work is well put together, it means that a thoughtful man planned it, and a careful man cut it, and an honest man cemented it. If it has too much ornament, it means that its carver was too greedy of pleasure; if too little, that he was rude, or insensitive, or stupid, and the like. So that when once you have learned how to spell these most precious of all legends,—pictures and buildings,—you may read the characters of men, and of nations, in their art, as in a mirror;—nay, as in a microscope, and magnified a hundredfold; for the character becomes passionate in the art, and intensifies itself in all its noblest or meanest delights. Nay, not only as in a microscope, but as under a scalpel, and in dissection; for a man may hide himself from you, or misrepresent himself to you, every other way; but he cannot in his work: there, be sure, you have him to the inmost. All that he likes, all that he sees,—all that he can do,—his imagination, his affections, his perseverance, his impatience, his clumsiness, cleverness, everything is there. If the work is a cobweb, you know it was made by a spider; if a honeycomb, by a bee; a worm-cast is thrown up by a worm, and a nest wreathed by a bird; and a house built by a man, worthily, if he is worthy, and ignobly, if he is ignoble.

And always, from the least to the greatest, as the made thing is good or bad, so is the maker of it.

103. You all use this faculty of judgment more or less, whether you theoretically admit the principle or not. Take that floral gable;* you don't suppose the man who built Stonehenge could have built that, or that the man

---

* The elaborate pediment above the central porch at the west end of Rouen Cathedral, pierced into a transparent web of tracery, and enriched with a border of "twisted eglantine."

who built that, *would* have built Stonehenge? Do you think an old Roman would have liked such a piece of filigree work? or that Michael Angelo would have spent his time in twisting these stems of roses in and out? Or, of modern handicraftsmen, do you think a burglar, or a brute, or a pickpocket could have carved it? Could Bill Sykes have done it? or the Dodger, dexterous with finger and tool? You will find in the end, that *no man could have done it but exactly the man who did it;* and by looking close at it, you may, if you know your letters, read precisely the manner of man he was.

104. Now I must insist on this matter, for a grave reason. Of all facts concerning art, this is the one most necessary to be known, that, while manufacture is the work of hands only, art is the work of the whole spirit of man; and as that spirit is, so is the deed of it: and by whatever power of vice or virtue any art is produced, the same vice or virtue it reproduces and teaches. That which is born of evil begets evil; and that which is born of valour and honour, teaches valour and honour. All art is either infection or education. It *must* be one or other of these.

105. This, I repeat, of all truths respecting art, is the one of which understanding is the most precious, and denial the most deadly. And I assert it the more, because it has of late been repeatedly, expressly, and with contumely, denied; and that by high authority: and I hold it one of the most sorrowful facts connected with the

decline of the arts among us, that English gentlemen, of high standing as scholars and artists, should have been blinded into the acceptance, and betrayed into the assertion of a fallacy which only authority such as theirs could have rendered for an instant credible. For the contrary of it is written in the history of all great nations; it is the one sentence always inscribed on the steps of their thrones; the one concordant voice in which they speak to us out of their dust.

All such nations first manifest themselves as a pure and beautiful animal race, with intense energy and imagination. They live lives of hardship by choice, and by grand instinct of manly discipline: they become fierce and irresistible soldiers; the nation is always its own army, and their king, or chief head of government, is always their first soldier. Pharaoh, or David, or Leonidas, or Valerius, or Barbarossa, or Cœur de Lion, or St. Louis, or Dandolo, or Frederick the Great:—Egyptian, Jew, Greek, Roman, German, English, French, Venetian,—that is inviolable law for them all; their king must be their first soldier, or they cannot be in progressive power. Then, after their great military period, comes the domestic period; in which, without betraying the discipline of war, they add to their great soldiership the delights and possessions of a delicate and tender home-life: and then, for all nations, is the time of their perfect art, which is the fruit, the evidence, the reward of their national ideal of character, developed by the finished care of the occupations of peace. That is the history of all true art that ever was, or can be : palpably the history of it,—unmistakeably,— written on the forehead of it in letters of light,—in tongues of fire, by which the seal of virtue is branded as deep as ever iron burnt into a convict's flesh the seal of crime. But always, hitherto, after the great period, has followed the day of luxury, and pursuit of the arts for pleasure only. And all has so ended.

106. Thus far of Abbeville building. Now I have here asserted two things,—first, the foundation of art in moral character; next, the foundation of moral character in war. I must make both these assertions clearer, and prove them.

First, of the foundation of art in moral character. Of course art-gift and amiability of disposition are two different things; a good man is not necessarily a painter, nor does an eye for colour necessarily imply an honest mind. But great art implies the union of both powers: it is the expression, by an art-gift, of a pure soul. If the gift is not there, we can have no art at all; and if the soul—and a right soul too—is not there, the art is bad, however dexterous.

107. But also, remember, that the art-gift itself is only the result of the moral character of generations. A bad woman may have a sweet voice; but that sweetness of voice comes of the past morality of her race. That she can sing with it at all, she owes to the determination of laws of music by the morality of the past. Every

act, every impulse, of virtue and vice, affects in any creature, face, voice, nervous power, and vigour and harmony of invention, at once. Perseverance in rightness of human conduct, renders, after a certain number of generations, human art possible; every sin clouds it, be it ever so little a one; and persistent vicious living and following of pleasure render, after a certain number of generations, all art impossible. Men are deceived by the long-suffering of the laws of nature; and mistake, in a nation, the reward of the virtue of its sires for the issue of its own sins. The time of their visitation will come, and that inevitably; for, it is always true, that if the fathers have eaten sour grapes, the children's teeth are set on edge. And for the individual, as soon as you have learned to read, you may, as I said, know him to the heart's core, through his art. Let his art-gift be never so great, and cultivated to the height by the schools of a great race of men; and it is still but a tapestry thrown over his own being and inner soul; and the bearing of it will show, infallibly, whether it hangs on a man, or on a skeleton. If you are dim-eyed, you may not see the difference in the fall of the folds at first, but learn how to look, and the folds themselves will become transparent, and you shall see through them the death's shape, or the divine one, making the tissue above it as a cloud of light, or as a winding-sheet.

108. Then farther, observe, I have said (and you will find it true, and that to the uttermost) that, as all lovely

art is rooted in virtue, so it bears fruit of virtue, and is didactic in its own nature. It is often didactic also in actually expressed thought, as Giotto's, Michael Angelo's, Durer's, and hundreds more; but that is not its special function,—it is didactic chiefly by being beautiful; but beautiful with haunting thought, no less than with form, and full of myths that can be read only with the heart.

For instance, at this moment there is open beside me as I write, a page of Persian manuscript, wrought with wreathed azure and gold, and soft green, and violet, and ruby and scarlet, into one field of pure resplendence. It is wrought to delight the eyes only; and does delight them; and the man who did it assuredly had eyes in his head; but not much more. It is not didactic art, but its author was happy: and it will do the good, and the harm, that mere pleasure can do. But, opposite me, is an early Turner drawing of the lake of Geneva, taken about two miles from Geneva, on the Lausanne road, with Mont Blanc in the distance. The old city is seen lying beyond the waveless waters, veiled with a sweet misty veil of Athena's weaving: a faint light of morning, peaceful exceedingly, and almost colourless, shed from behind the Voirons, increases into soft amber along the slope of the Saleve, and is just seen, and no more, on the fair warm fields of its summit, between the folds of a white cloud that rests upon the grass, but rises, high and tower-like, into the zenith of dawn above.

109. There is not as much colour in that low amber light upon the hill-side as there is in the palest dead leaf. The lake is not blue, but gray in mist, passing into deep shadow beneath the Voirons' pines; a few dark clusters of leaves, a single white flower—scarcely seen—are all the gladness given to the rocks of the shore. One of the ruby spots of the eastern manuscript would give colour enough for all the red that is in Turner's entire drawing. For the mere pleasure of the eye, there is not so much in all those lines of his, throughout the entire landscape, as in half an inch square of the Persian's page. What made him take pleasure in the low colour that is only like the brown of a dead leaf? in the cold gray of dawn—in the one white flower among the rocks—in these—and no more than these?

110. He took pleasure in them because he had been bred among English fields and hills; because the gentleness of a great race was in his heart, and its powers of thought in his brain; because he knew the stories of the Alps, and of the cities at their feet; because he had read the Homeric legends of the clouds, and beheld the gods of dawn, and the givers of dew to the fields; because he knew the faces of the crags, and the imagery of the passionate mountains, as a man knows the face of his friend; because he had in him the wonder and sorrow concerning life and death, which are the inheritance of the Gothic soul from the days of its first sea kings; and also the compassion and the joy that are woven into the innermost fabric of every great imaginative spirit, born now in

countries that have lived by the Christian faith with any courage or truth. And the picture contains also, for us, just this which its maker had in him to give; and can convey it to us, just so far as we are of the temper in which it must be received. It is didactic if we are worthy to be taught, no otherwise. The pure heart, it will make more pure; the thoughtful, more thoughtful. It has in it no words for the reckless or the base.

111. As I myself look at it, there is no fault nor folly of my life,—and both have been many and great,—that does not rise up against me, and take away my joy, and shorten my power of possession, of sight, of understanding. And every past effort of my life, every gleam of rightness or good in it, is with me now, to help me in my grasp of this art, and its vision. So far as I can rejoice in, or interpret either, my power is owing to what of right there is in me. I dare to say it, that, because through all my life I have desired good, and not evil; because I have been kind to many; have wished to be kind to all; have wilfully injured none; and because I have loved much, and not selfishly; —therefore, the morning light is yet visible to me on those hills, and you, who read, may trust my thought and word in such work as I have to do for you; and you will be glad afterwards that you have trusted them.

112. Yet remember,—I repeat it again and yet again,— that I may for once, if possible, make this thing assuredly clear:—the inherited art-gift must be there, as well as the life in some poor measure, or rescued fragment, right.

This art-gift of mine could not have been won by any work, or by any conduct: it belongs to me by birthright, and came by Athena's will, from the air of English country villages, and Scottish hills. I will risk whatever charge of folly may come on me, for printing one of my many childish rhymes, written on a frosty day in Glen Farg, just north of Loch Leven. It bears date 1st January, 1828. I was born on the 8th of February, 1819; and all that I ever could be, and all that I cannot be, the weak little rhyme already shows.

> "Papa, how pretty those icicles are,
> That are seen so near,—that are seen so far;
> —Those dropping waters that come from the rocks
> And many a hole, like the haunt of a fox.
> That silvery stream that runs babbling along,
> Making a murmuring, dancing song.
> Those trees that stand waving upon the rock's side,
> And men, that, like spectres, among them glide.
> And waterfalls that are heard from far,
> And come in sight when very near.
> And the water-wheel that turns slowly round,
> Grinding the corn that—requires to be ground,—

(Political Economy of the future!)

> ——And mountains at a distance seen,
> And rivers winding through the plain.
> And quarries with their craggy stones,
> And the wind among them moans."

So foretelling Stones of Venice, and this essay on **Athena**. Enough now concerning myself.

113. Of Turner's life, and of its good and evil, both great, but the good immeasurably the greater, his work is in all things a perfect and transparent evidence. His biography is simply,—" He did this, nor will ever another do its like again." Yet read what I have said of him, as compared with the great Italians, in the passages taken from the " Cestus of Aglaia," farther on, § 158, p. 162.

114. This then is the nature of the connection of morals with art. Now, secondly, I have asserted the foundation of both these, at least, hitherto, in war. The reason of this too manifest fact is, that, until now, it has been impossible for any nation, except a warrior one, to fix its mind wholly on its men, instead of on their possessions. Every great soldier nation thinks, necessarily, first of multiplying its bodies and souls of men, in good temper and strict discipline. As long as this is its political aim, it does not matter what it temporarily suffers, or loses, either in numbers or in wealth; its morality and its arts, (if it have national art-gift,) advance together; but so soon as it ceases to be a warrior nation, it thinks of its possessions instead of its men; and then the moral and poetic powers vanish together.

115. It is thus, however, absolutely necessary to the virtue of war that it should be waged by personal strength, not by money or machinery. A nation that fights with a mercenary force, or with torpedos instead of its own arms, is dying. Not but that there is more true courage in modern than even in ancient war; but this is, first, because all

the remaining life of European nations is with a morbid intensity thrown into their soldiers ; and, secondly, because their present heroism is the culmination of centuries of inbred and traditional valour, which Athena taught them by forcing them to govern the foam of the sea-wave and of the horse,—not the steam of kettles.

116. And farther, note this, which is vital to us in the present crisis : If war is to be made by money and machinery, the nation which is the largest and most covetous multitude will win. You may be as scientific as you choose ; the mob that can pay more for sulphuric acid and gunpowder will at last poison its bullets, throw acid in your faces, and make an end of you ;—of itself, also, in good time, but of you first. And to the English people the choice of its fate is very near now. It may spasmodically defend its property with iron walls a fathom thick, a few years longer—a very few. No walls will defend either it, or its havings, against the multitude that is breeding and spreading, faster than the clouds, over the habitable earth. We shall be allowed to live by small pedlar's business, and ironmongery—since we have chosen those for our line of life—as long as we are found useful black servants to the Americans ; and are content to dig coals and sit in the cinders ; and have still coals to dig,—they once exhausted, or got cheaper elsewhere, we shall be abolished. But if we think more wisely, while there is yet time, and set our minds again on multiplying Englishmen, and not on cheapening English wares ; if we resolve to submit to

wholesome laws of labour and economy, and, setting our political squabbles aside, try how many strong creatures, friendly and faithful to each other, we can crowd into every spot of English dominion, neither poison nor iron will prevail against us; nor traffic—nor hatred: the noble nation will yet by the grace of Heaven, rule over the ignoble, and force of heart hold its own against fire-balls.

117. But there is yet a farther reason for the dependence of the arts on war. The vice and injustice of the world are constantly springing anew, and are only to be subdued by battle; the keepers of order and law must always be soldiers. And now, going back to the myth of Athena, we see that though she is first a warrior maid, she detests war for its own sake; she arms Achilles and Ulysses in just quarrels, but she *disarms* Ares. She contends, herself, continually against disorder and convulsion, in the Earth giants; she stands by Hercules' side in victory over all monstrous evil: in justice only she judges and makes war. But in this war of hers she is wholly implacable. She has little notion of converting criminals. There is no faculty of mercy in her when she has been resisted. Her word is only, " I will mock when your fear cometh." Note the words that follow: " when your fear cometh as desolation, and your destruction as a whirlwind;" for her wrath is of irresistible tempest: once roused, it is blind and deaf,—rabies—madness of anger—darkness of the Dies Iræ.

And that is, indeed, the sorrowfullest fact we have to

know about our own several lives. Wisdom never forgives. Whatever resistance we have offered to her law, she avenges for ever;—the lost hour can never be redeemed, and the accomplished wrong never atoned for. The best that can be done afterwards, but for that, had been better;—the falsest of all the cries of peace, where there is no peace, is that of the pardon of sin, as the mob expect it. Wisdom can "put away" sin, but she cannot pardon it; and she is apt, in her haste, to put away the sinner as well, when the black ægis is on her breast.

118. And this is also a fact we have to know about our national life, that it is ended as soon as it has lost the power of noble Anger. When it paints over, and apologizes for its pitiful criminalities; and endures its false weights, and its adulterated food;—dares not to decide practically between good and evil, and can neither honour the one, nor smite the other, but sneers at the good, as if it were hidden evil, and consoles the evil with pious sympathy, and conserves it in the sugar of its leaden heart,—the end is come.

119. The first sign, then, of Athena's presence with any people, is that they become warriors, and that the chief thought of every man of them is to stand rightly in his rank, and not fail from his brother's side in battle. Wealth, and pleasure, and even love, are all, under Athena's orders, sacrificed to this duty of standing fast in the rank of war.

But farther: Athena presides over industry, as well as

battle; typically, over women's industry; that brings comfort with pleasantness. Her word to us all is:—"Be well exercised, and rightly clothed. Clothed, and in your right minds; not insane and in rags, nor in soiled fine clothes clutched from each other's shoulders. Fight and weave. Then I myself will answer for the course of the lance, and the colours of the loom."

And now I will ask the reader to look with some care through these following passages respecting modern multitudes and their occupations, written long ago, but left in fragmentary form, in which they must now stay, and be of what use they can.

120. It is not political economy to put a number of strong men down on an acre of ground, with no lodging, and nothing to eat. Nor is it political economy to build a city on good ground, and fill it with store of corn and treasure, and put a score of lepers to live in it. Political economy creates together the means of life, and the living persons who are to use them; and of both, the best and the most that it can, but imperatively the best, not the most. A few good and healthy men, rather than a multitude of diseased rogues; and a little real milk and wine rather than much chalk and petroleum; but the gist of the whole business is that the men and their property must both be produced together—not one to the loss of the other. Property must not be created in lands desolate by exile of their people, nor multiplied and depraved humanity, in lands barren of bread.

121. Nevertheless, though the men and their possessions are to be increased at the same time, the first object of thought is always to be the multiplication of a worthy people. The strength of the nation is in its multitude, not in its territory; but only in its sound multitude. It is one thing, both in a man and a nation, to gain flesh, and another to be swollen with putrid humours. Not that multitude ever ought to be inconsistent with virtue. Two men should be wiser than one, and two thousand than two; nor do I know another so gross fallacy in the records of human stupidity as that excuse for neglect of crime by greatness of cities. As if the first purpose of congregation were not to devise laws and repress crimes! as if bees and wasps could live honestly in flocks,—men, only in separate dens!—as if it was easy to help one another on the opposite sides of a mountain, and impossible on the opposite sides of a street! But when the men are true and good, and stand shoulder to shoulder, the strength of any nation is in its quantity of life, not in its land nor gold. The more good men a state has, in proportion to its territory, the stronger the state. And as it has been the madness of economists to seek for gold instead of life, so it has been the madness of kings to seek for land instead of life. They want the town on the other side of the river, and seek it at the spear point: it never enters their stupid heads that to double the honest souls in the town on *this* side of the river, would make them stronger kings; and that this doubling might be done by the ploughshare in-

stead of the spear, and through happiness instead of misery.

Therefore, in brief, this is the object of all true policy and true economy: "utmost multitude of good men on every given space of ground"—imperatively always, good, sound, honest men, not a mob of white-faced thieves. So that, on the one hand, all aristocracy is wrong which is inconsistent with numbers; and, on the other, all numbers are wrong which are inconsistent with breeding.

122. Then, touching the accumulation of wealth for the maintenance of such men, observe, that you must never use the terms "money" and "wealth" as synonymous. Wealth consists of the good, and therefore useful, things in the possession of the nation: money is only the written or coined sign of the relative quantities of wealth in each person's possession. All money is a divisible title-deed, of immense importance as an expression of right to property; but absolutely valueless, as property itself. Thus, supposing a nation isolated from all others, the money in its possession is, at its maximum value, worth all the property of the nation, and no more, because no more can be got for it. And the money of all nations is worth, at its maximum, the property of all nations, and no more, for no more can be got for it. Thus, every article of property produced increases, by its value, the value of all the money in the world, and every article of property destroyed, diminishes the value of all the money in the world. If ten men are cast away on a rock, with a thousand pounds

in their pockets, and there is on the rock neither food nor shelter, their money is worth simply nothing; for nothing is to be had for it: if they build ten huts, and recover a cask of biscuit from the wreck, then their thousand pounds, at its maximum value, is worth ten huts and a cask of biscuit. If they make their thousand pounds into two thousand by writing new notes, their two thousand pounds are still only worth ten huts and a cask of biscuit. And the law of relative value is the same for all the world, and all the people in it, and all their property, as for ten men on a rock. Therefore, money is truly and finally lost in the degree in which its value is taken from it, (ceasing in that degree to be money at all); and it is truly gained in the degree in which value is added to it. Thus, suppose the money coined by the nation to be a fixed sum, divided very minutely, (say into francs and cents), and neither to be added to, nor diminished. Then every grain of food and inch of lodging added to its possessions makes every cent in its pockets worth proportionally more, and every grain of food it consumes, and inch of roof it allows to fall to ruin, makes every cent in its pockets worth less; and this with mathematical precision. The immediate value of the money at particular times and places depends, indeed, on the humours of the possessors of property; but the nation is in the one case gradually getting richer; and will feel the pressure of poverty steadily everywhere relaxing, whatever the humours of individuals may be; and, in the other case, is gradually growing poorer, and the pressure of its poverty will every day tell more and more, in ways that it cannot explain, but will most bitterly feel.

123. The actual quantity of money which it coins, in relation to its real property, is therefore only of consequence for convenience of exchange; but the proportion in which this quantity of money is divided among individuals expresses their various rights to greater or less proportions of the national property, and must not, therefore, be tampered with. The Government may at any time, with perfect justice, double its issue of coinage, if it gives every man who had ten pounds in his pocket, another ten pounds, and every man who had ten pence, another ten pence; for it thus does not make any of them richer; it merely divides their counters for them into twice the number. But if it gives the newly-issued coins to other people, or keeps them itself, it simply robs the former holders to precisely that extent. This most important function of money, as a title-deed, on the non-violation of which all national soundness of commerce and peace of life depend, has been never rightly distinguished by economists from the quite unimportant function of money as a means of exchange. You can exchange goods,—at some inconvenience, indeed, but still you can contrive to do it,—without money at all; but you cannot maintain your claim to the savings of your past life without a document declaring the amount of them, which the nation and its Government will respect.

124. And as economists have lost sight of this great function of money in relation to individual rights, so they have equally lost sight of its function as a representative of good things. That, for every good thing produced, so much money is put into everybody's pocket—is the one simple and primal truth for the public to know, and for economists to teach. How many of them have taught it? Some have; but only incidentally; and others will say it is a truism. If it be, do the public know it? Does your ordinary English householder know that every costly dinner he gives has destroyed for ever as much money as it is worth? Does every well-educated girl—do even the women in high political position—know that every fine dress they wear themselves, or cause to be worn, destroys precisely so much of the national money as the labour and material of it are worth? If this be a truism, it is one that needs proclaiming somewhat louder.

125. That, then, is the relation of money and goods. So much goods, so much money; so little goods, so little money. But, as there is this true relation between money and "goods," or good things, so there is a false relation between money and "bads," or bad things. Many bad things will fetch a price in exchange; but they do not increase the wealth of the country. Good wine is wealth—drugged wine is not; good meat is wealth—putrid meat is not; good pictures are wealth—bad pictures are not. A thing is worth precisely what

it can do for you; not what you choose to pay for it. You may pay a thousand pounds for a cracked pipkin, if you please; but you do not by that transaction make the cracked pipkin worth one that will hold water, nor that, nor any pipkin whatsoever, worth more than it was before you paid such sum for it. You may, perhaps, induce many potters to manufacture fissured pots, and many amateurs of clay to buy them; but the nation is, through the whole business so encouraged, rich by the addition to its wealth of so many potsherds—and there an end. The thing is worth what it CAN do for you, not what you think it can; and most national luxuries, now-a-days, are a form of potsherd, provided for the solace of a self-complacent Job, voluntary sedent on his ash-heap.

126. And, also, so far as good things already exist, and have become media of exchange, the variations in their prices are absolutely indifferent to the nation. Whether Mr. A. buys a Titian from Mr. B. for twenty, or for two thousand, pounds, matters not sixpence to the national revenue: that is to say, it matters in nowise to the revenue whether Mr. A. has the picture, and Mr. B. the money, or Mr. B. the picture, and Mr. A. the money. Which of them will spend the money most wisely, and which of them will keep the picture most carefully, is, indeed, a matter of some importance; but this cannot be known by the mere fact of exchange.

127. The wealth of a nation then, first, and its peace and well-being besides, depend on the number of persons

it can employ in making good and useful things. I say its well-being also, for the character of men depends more on their occupations than on any teaching we can give them, or principles with which we can imbue them. The employment forms the habits of body and mind, and these are the constitution of the man;—the greater part of his moral or persistent nature, whatever effort, under special excitement, he may make to change, or overcome them. Employment is the half, and the primal half, of education—it is the warp of it; and the fineness or the endurance of all subsequently woven pattern depends wholly on its straightness and strength. And, whatever difficulty there may be in tracing through past history the remoter connections of event and cause, one chain of sequence is always clear: the formation, namely, of the character of nations by their employments, and the determination of their final fate by their character. The moment, and the first direction of decisive revolutions, often depend on accident; but their persistent course, and their consequences, depend wholly on the nature of the people. The passing of the Reform Bill by the late English Parliament may have been more or less accidental: the results of the measure now rest on the character of the English people, as it has been developed by their recent interests, occupations, and habits of life. Whether, as a body, they employ their new powers for good or evil, will depend, not on their facilities of knowledge, nor even on the general intelligence they may possess; but on the number of persons among them whom wholesome employments have rendered familiar with the duties, and modest in their estimate of the promises, of Life.

128. But especially in framing laws respecting the treatment or employment of improvident and more or less vicious persons, it is to be remembered that as men are not made heroes by the performance of an act of heroism, but must be brave before they can perform it, so they are not made villains by the commission of a crime, but were villains before they committed it; and that the right of public interference with their conduct begins when they begin to corrupt themselves;—not merely at the moment when they have proved themselves hopelessly corrupt.

All measures of reformation are effective in exact proportion to their timeliness: partial decay may be cut away and cleansed; incipient error corrected: but there is a point at which corruption can no more be stayed, nor wandering recalled. It has been the manner of modern philanthropy to remain passive until that precise period, and to leave the sick to perish, and the foolish to stray, while it spent itself in frantic exertions to raise the dead, and reform the dust.

The recent direction of a great weight of public opinion against capital punishment is, I trust, the sign of an awakening perception that punishment is the last and worst instrument in the hands of the legislator for the prevention of crime. The true instruments of reformation are employment and reward;—not punishment. Aid the willing, honour the virtuous, and compel the idle into occupation, and there will be no need for the compelling of any into the great and last indolence of death.

129. The beginning of all true reformation among the criminal classes depends on the establishment of institutions for their active employment, while their criminality is still unripe, and their feelings of self-respect, capacities of affection, and sense of justice, not altogether quenched. That those who are desirous of employment should always be able to find it, will hardly, at the present day, be disputed: but that those who are *un*desirous of employment should of all persons be the most strictly compelled to it, the public are hardly yet convinced; and they must be convinced. If the danger of the principal thoroughfares in their capital city, and the multiplication of crimes more ghastly than ever yet disgraced a nominal civilization, are not enough, they will not have to wait long before they receive sterner lessons. For our neglect of the lower orders has reached a point at which it begins to bear its necessary fruit, and every day makes the fields, not whiter, but more sable, to harvest.

130. The general principles by which employment should be regulated may be briefly stated as follows:—

1. There being three great classes of mechanical powers at our disposal, namely, (*a*) vital or muscular power;

(*b*) natural mechanical power of wind, water, and electricity; and (*c*) artificially produced mechanical power; it is the first principle of economy to use all available vital power first, then the inexpensive natural forces, and only at last to have recourse to artificial power. And this, because it is always better for a man to work with his own hands to feed and clothe himself, than to stand idle while a machine works for him; and if he cannot by all the labour healthily possible to him, feed and clothe himself, then it is better to use an inexpensive machine—as a windmill or watermill—than a costly one like a steam-engine, so long as we have natural force enough at our disposal. Whereas at present we continually hear economists regret that the water-power of the cascades or streams of a country should be lost, but hardly ever that the muscular power of its idle inhabitants should be lost; and, again, we see vast districts, as the south of Provence, where a strong wind* blows steadily all day long for six days out of seven throughout the year, without a windmill, while men are continually employed a hundred miles to the north, in digging fuel to obtain artificial power. But the principal point of all to be kept in view is, that in every idle arm and shoulder throughout the country there is a certain quantity of force, equivalent to the force of so much fuel; and that it is mere insane

* In order fully to utilize this natural power, we only require machinery to turn the variable into a constant velocity—no insurmountable difficulty.

waste to dig for coal for our force, while the vital force is unused; and not only unused, but, in being so, corrupting and polluting itself. We waste our coal, and spoil our humanity at one and the same instant. Therefore, wherever there is an idle arm, always save coal with it, and the stores of England will last all the longer. And precisely the same argument answers the common one about " taking employment out of the hands of the industrious labourer." Why, what is " employment " but the putting out of vital force instead of mechanical force? We are continually in search of means of strength,—to pull,-to hammer, to fetch, to carry; we waste our future resources to get this strength, while we leave all the living fuel to burn itself out in mere pestiferous breath, and production of its variously noisome forms of ashes! Clearly, if we want fire for force, we want men for force first. The industrious hands must already have so much to do that they can do no more, or else we need not use machines to help them. Then use the idle hands first. Instead of dragging petroleum with a steam-engine, put it on a canal, and drag it with human arms and shoulders. Petroleum cannot possibly be in a hurry to arrive anywhere. We can always order that, and many other things, time enough before we want it. So, the carriage of everything which does not spoil by keeping may most wholesomely and safely be done by water-traction and sailing vessels; and no healthier work can men be put to, nor better discipline, than such active porterage.

131. (2nd.) In employing all the muscular power at our disposal we are to make the employments we choose as educational as possible. For a wholesome human employment is the first and best method of education, mental as well as bodily. A man taught to plough, row, or steer well, and a woman taught to cook properly, and make a dress neatly, are already educated in many essential moral habits. Labour considered as a discipline has hitherto been thought of only for criminals; but the real and noblest function of labour is to prevent crime, and not to be *R*eformatory, but Formatory.

132. The third great principle of employment is, that whenever there is pressure of poverty to be met, all enforced occupation should be directed to the production of useful articles only, that is to say, of food, of simple clothing, of lodging, or of the means of conveying, distributing, and preserving these. It is yet little understood by economists, and not at all by the public, that the employment of persons in a useless business cannot relieve ultimate distress. The money given to employ riband-makers at Coventry is merely so much money withdrawn from what would have employed lace-makers at Honiton: or makers of something else, as useless, elsewhere. We *must* spend our money in some way, at some time, and it cannot at any time be spent without employing somebody. If we gamble it away, the person who wins it must spend it; if we lose it in a railroad speculation, it has gone into some one else's

pockets, or merely gone to pay navvies for making a useless embankment, instead of to pay riband or button makers for making useless ribands or buttons; we cannot lose it (unless by actually destroying it) without giving employment of some kind; and therefore, whatever quantity of money exists, the relative quantity of employment must some day come out of it; but the distress of the nation signifies that the employments given have produced nothing that will support its existence. Men cannot live on ribands, or buttons, or velvet, or by going quickly from place to place; and every coin spent in useless ornament, or useless motion, is so much withdrawn from the national means of life. One of the most beautiful uses of railroads is to enable A to travel from the town of X to take away the business of B in the town of Y; while, in the meantime, B travels from the town of Y to take away A's business in the town of X. But the national wealth is not increased by these operations. Whereas every coin spent in cultivating ground, in repairing lodging, in making necessary and good roads, in preventing danger by sea or land, and in carriage of food or fuel where they are required, is so much absolute and direct gain to the whole nation. To cultivate land round Coventry makes living easier at Honiton, and every acre of sand gained from the sea in Lincolnshire, makes life easier all over England.

4th, and lastly. Since for every idle person, some one else must be working somewhere to provide him with clothes and food, and doing, therefore, double the quantity of work that would be enough for his own needs, it is only a matter of pure justice to compel the idle person to work for his maintenance himself. The conscription has been used in many countries, to take away labourers who supported their families, from their useful work, and maintain them for purposes chiefly of military display at the public expense. Since this has been long endured by the most civilized nations, let it not be thought that they would not much more gladly endure a conscription which should seize only the vicious and idle, already living by criminal procedures at the public expense; and which should discipline and educate them to labour which would not only maintain themselves, but be serviceable to the commonwealth. The question is simply this:—we *must* feed the drunkard, vagabond, and thief;—but shall we do so by letting them steal their food, and do no work for it? or shall we give them their food in appointed quantity, and enforce their doing work which shall be worth it? and which, in process of time, will redeem their own characters, and make them happy and serviceable members of society?

I find by me a violent little fragment of undelivered lecture, which puts this, perhaps, still more clearly. Your idle people, (it says,) as they are now, are not merely waste coal-beds. They are explosive coal-beds, which you pay a high annual rent for. You are keeping all these idle persons, remember, at far greater cost than if they were busy. Do you think a vicious person eats less than an honest one? or that it is cheaper to keep a bad man drunk, than a good man sober? There is, I suppose, a dim idea in the mind of the public, that they don't pay for the maintenance of people they don't employ. Those staggering rascals at the street corner, grouped around its splendid angle of public-house, we fancy they are no servants of ours? that we pay them no wages? that no cash out of our pockets is spent over that beer-stained counter!

Whose cash is it then they are spending? It is not got honestly by work. You know that much. Where do they get it from? Who has paid for their dinner and their pot? Those fellows can only live in one of two ways—by pillage or beggary. Their annual income by thieving comes out of the public pocket, you will admit. They are not cheaply fed, so far as they are fed by theft. But the rest of their living—all that they don't steal— they must beg. Not with success from you, you think. Wise as benevolent, you never gave a penny in "indiscriminate charity." Well, I congratulate you on the freedom of your conscience from that sin, mine being bitterly burdened with the memory of many a sixpence given to beggars of whom I knew nothing, but that they had pale faces and thin waists. But it is not that kind of street beggary that the vagabonds of our people chiefly practise. It is home beggary that is the worst beggars' trade. Home alms which it is their worst degradation to receive. Those scamps know well enough that you and your wisdom are worth nothing to them. They won't beg of you. They will beg of their sisters, and mothers, and wives, and children, and of any one else who is enough ashamed of being of the same blood with them to pay to keep them out of sight. Every one of those blackguards is the bane of a family. *That* is the deadly "indiscriminate charity"—the charity which each household pays to maintain its own private curse.

133. And you think that is no affair of yours? and that every family ought to watch over and subdue its own living plague? Put it to yourselves this way, then: suppose you knew every one of those families kept an idol in an inner room—a big-bellied bronze figure, to which daily sacrifice and oblation was made; at whose feet so much beer and brandy was poured out every morning on the ground: and before which, every night, good meat, enough for two men's keep, was set, and left, till it was putrid, and then carried out and thrown on the dunghill;—you would put an end to that form of idolatry with your best diligence, I suppose. You would understand then that the beer, and brandy, and meat, were wasted; and that the burden imposed by each household on itself lay heavily through them on the whole community? But, suppose farther, that this idol were not of silent and quiet bronze only;—but an ingenious mechanism, wound up every morning, to run itself down in automatic blasphemies; that it struck and tore with its hands the people who set food

before it; that it was anointed with poisonous unguents, and infected the air for miles round. You would interfere with the idolatry then, straightway? Will you not interfere with it now, when the infection that the venomous idol spreads is not merely death—but sin?

134. So far the old lecture. Returning to cool English, the end of the matter is, that sooner or later, we shall have to register our people; and to know how they live; and to make sure, if they are capable of work, that right work is given them to do.

The different classes of work for which bodies of men could be consistently organized, might ultimately become numerous; these following divisions of occupation may at once be suggested:—

1. *Road-making.*—Good roads to be made, wherever needed, and kept in repair; and the annual loss on unfrequented roads, in spoiled horses, strained wheels, and time, done away with.

2. *Bringing in of waste land.*—All waste lands not necessary for public health, to be made accessible and gradually reclaimed; chiefly our wide and waste seashores. Not our mountains nor moorland. Our life depends on them, more than on the best arable we have.

3. *Harbour-making.*—The deficiencies of safe or convenient harbourage in our smaller ports to be remedied; other harbours built at dangerous points of coast, and a disciplined body of men always kept in connection with the pilot and life-boat services. There is room for every order

of intelligence in this work, and for a large body of superior officers.

4. *Porterage.*—All heavy goods, not requiring speed in transit, to be carried (under preventive duty on transit by railroad) by canal-boats, employing men for draught; and the merchant-shipping service extended by sea; so that no ships may be wrecked for want of hands, while there are idle ones in mischief on shore.

5. *Repair of buildings.*—A body of men in various trades to be kept at the disposal of the authorities in every large town, for repair of buildings, especially the houses of the poorer orders, who, if no such provision were made, could not employ workmen on their own houses, but would simply live with rent walls and roofs.

6. *Dressmaking.*—Substantial dress, of standard material and kind, strong shoes, and stout bedding, to be manufactured for the poor, so as to render it unnecessary for them, unless by extremity of improvidence, to wear cast clothes, or be without sufficiency of clothing.

7. *Works of Art.*—Schools to be established on thoroughly sound principles of manufacture, and use of materials, and with sample and, for given periods, unalterable modes of work; first, in pottery, and embracing gradually metal work, sculpture, and decorative painting; the two points insisted upon, in distinction from ordinary commercial establishments, being perfectness of material to the utmost attainable degree; and the production of everything by hand-work, for the special

purpose of developing personal power and skill in the workman.

The two last departments, and some subordinate branches of the others, would include the service of women and children.

I give now, for such farther illustration as they contain of the points I desire most to insist upon with respect both to education and employment, a portion of the series of notes published some time ago in the *Art Journal*, on the opposition of Modesty and Liberty, and the unescapable law of wise restraint. I am sorry that they are written obscurely;—and it may be thought affectedly:—but the fact is, I have always had three different ways of writing; one, with the single view of making myself understood, in which I necessarily omit a great deal of what comes into my head:—another, in which I say what I think ought to be said, in what I suppose to be the best words I can find for it; (which is in reality an affected style—be it good or bad;) and my third way of writing is to say all that comes into my head for my own pleasure, in the first words that come, retouching them afterwards into (approximate) grammar. These notes for the *Art Journal* were so written; and I like them myself, of course; but ask the reader's pardon for their confusedness.

135. "Sir, it cannot be better done."

We will insist, with the reader's permission, on this comfortful saying of Albert Durer's, in order to find out, if we may, what Modesty is; which it will be well for painters, readers, and especially critics, to know, before going farther. What it is ; or, rather, who she is ; her fingers being among the deftest in laying the ground-threads of Aglaia's Cestus.

For this same opinion of Albert's is entertained by many other people respecting their own doings—a very prevalent opinion, indeed, I find it ; and the answer itself, though rarely made with the Nuremberger's crushing decision, is nevertheless often enough intimated, with delicacy, by artists of all countries, in their various dialects. Neither can it always be held an entirely modest one, as it assuredly was in the man who would sometimes estimate a piece of his unconquerable work at only the worth of a plate of fruit, or a flask of wine—would have taken even one " fig for it," kindly offered ; or given it royally for nothing, to show his hand to a fellow-king of his own, or any other craft—as Gainsborough gave the " Boy at the Stile " for a solo on the violin. An entirely modest saying, I repeat, in him—not always in us. For Modesty is " the measuring virtue," the virtue of *modes* or limits. She is, indeed, said to be only the third or youngest of the children of the cardinal virtue, Temperance ; and apt to be despised, being more given to arithmetic, and other vulgar studies (Cinderella-like) than her elder sisters : but she is useful in the household, and arrives at great results with her yard-measure and slate-pencil—a pretty little Marchande des Modes, cutting her dress always according to the silk (if this be the proper feminine reading of " coat according to the cloth "), so that, consulting with her carefully of a morning, men get to know not only their income, but their inbeing—to know *themselves*, that is, in a gauger's manner, round, and up and down—surface and contents; what is in them, and what may be got out of them; and, in fine, their entire canon of weight and capacity. That yard-measure of Modesty's, lent to those who will use it, is a curious musical reed, and will go round and round waists that are slender enough, with latent melody in every joint of it, the dark root only being soundless, moist from the wave wherein

"Null' altra pianta che facesse fronda
O indurasse, puote aver vita."*

But when the little sister herself takes it in hand, to measure things outside of us with, the joints shoot out in an amazing manner: the four-square walls even of celestial cities being measurable enough by that reed; and the way pointed to them, though only to be followed, or even seen, in the dim starlight shed down from worlds amidst which there is no name of Measure any more, though the reality of it always. For, indeed, to all true modesty the necessary business is not inlook, but outlook, and especially *up*-look: it is only her sister, Shamefacedness, who is known by the drooping lashes—Modesty, quite otherwise, by her large eyes full of wonder; for she never contemns herself, nor is ashamed of herself, but forgets herself—at least until she has done something worth memory. It is easy to

* *Purgatorio*, i. 103.

peep and potter about one's own deficiencies in a quiet immodest discontent; but Modesty is so pleased with other people's doings, that she has no leisure to lament her own: and thus, knowing the fresh feeling of contentment, unstained with thought of self, she does not fear being pleased, when there is cause, with her own rightness, as with another's, saying calmly, "Be it mine, or yours, or whose else's it may, it is no matter;—this also is well." But the right to say such a thing depends on continual reverence, and manifold sense of failure. If you have known yourself to have failed, you may trust, when it comes, the strange consciousness of success; if you have faithfully loved the noble work of others, you need not fear to speak with respect of things duly done, of your own.

136. But the principal good that comes of art's being followed in this reverent feeling, is vitally manifest in the associative conditions of it. Men who know their place, can take it and keep it, be it low or high, contentedly and firmly, neither yielding nor grasping; and the harmony of hand and thought follows, rendering all great deeds of art possible—deeds in which the souls of men meet like the jewels in the windows of Aladdin's palace, the little gems and the large all equally pure, needing no cement but the fitting of facets; while the associative work of immodest men is all jointless, and astir with wormy ambition; putridly dissolute, and for ever on the crawl: so that if it come together for a time, it can only be by me-

tamorphosis through flash of volcanic fire out of the vale of Siddim, vitrifying the clay of it, and fastening the slime, only to end in wilder scattering; according to the fate of those oldest, mightiest, immodestest of builders, of whom it is told in scorn, "They had brick for stone, and slime had they for mortar."

137. The first function of Modesty, then, being this recognition of place, her second is the recognition of law, and delight in it, for the sake of law itself, whether her part be to assert it, or obey. For as it belongs to all immodesty to defy or deny law, and assert privilege and licence, according to its own pleasure (it being therefore rightly called "in*solent*," that is, "custom-breaking," violating some usual and appointed order to attain for itself greater forwardness or power), so it is the habit of all modesty to love the constancy and "*solem*nity," or, literally, "accustomedness," of law, seeking first what are the solemn, appointed, inviolable customs and general orders of nature, and of the Master of nature, touching the matter in hand; and striving to put itself, as habitually and inviolably, in compliance with them. Out of which habit, once established, arises what is rightly called "conscience," not "science" merely, but "with-science," a science "with us," such as only modest creatures can have—with or within them—and within all creation besides, every member of it, strong or weak, witnessing together, and joining in the happy consciousness that each one's work is good; the bee also being profoundly of that

opinion; and the lark; and the swallow, in that noisy, but modestly upside-down, Babel of hers, under the eaves, with its unvolcanic slime for mortar; and the two ants who are asking of each other at the turn of that little ant's-foot-worn path through the moss, "lor via e lor fortuna;" and the builders also, who built yonder pile of cloud-marble in the west, and the gilder who gilded it, and is gone down behind it.

138. But I think we shall better understand what we ought of the nature of Modesty, and of her opposite, by taking a simple instance of both, in the practice of that art of music which the wisest have agreed in thinking the first element of education; only I must ask the reader's patience with me through a parenthesis.

Among the foremost men whose power has had to assert itself, though with conquest, yet with countless loss, through peculiarly English disadvantages of circumstance, are assuredly to be ranked together, both for honour and for mourning, Thomas Bewick and George Cruikshank. There is, however, less cause for regret in the instance of Bewick. We may understand that it was well for us once to see what an entirely powerful painter's genius, and an entirely keen and true man's temper, could achieve, together, unhelped, but also unharmed, among the black banks and wolds of Tyne. But the genius of Cruikshank has been cast away in an utterly ghastly and lamentable manner: his superb line-work, worthy of any class of subject, and his powers of conception and composition, of which I cannot venture to estimate the range in their degraded application, having been condemned, by his fate, to be spent either in rude jesting, or in vain war with conditions of vice too low alike for record or rebuke, among the dregs of the British populace. Yet perhaps I am wrong in regretting even this: it may be an appointed lesson for futurity, that the art of the best English etcher in the nineteenth century, spent on illustrations of the lives of burglars and drunkards, should one day be seen in museums beneath Greek-vases fretted with drawings of the wars of Troy, or side by side with Durer's "Knight and Death."

139. Be that as it may, I am at present glad to be able to refer to one of these perpetuations, by his strong hand, of such human character as our faultless British constitution occasionally produces, in out-of-the-way corners. It is among his illustrations of the Irish Rebellion, and represents the pillage and destruction of a gentleman's house by the mob. They have made a heap in the drawing-room of the furniture and books, to set first fire to; and are tearing up the floor for its more easily kindled planks: the less busily-disposed meanwhile hacking round in rage, with axes, and smashing what they can with butt-ends of guns. I do not care to follow with words the ghastly truth of the picture into its detail; but the most expressive incident of the whole, and the one immediately to my purpose, is this, that one fellow has sat himself at the piano, on which, hitting down fiercely with his clenched

fists, he plays, grinning, such tune as may be so producible, to which melody two of his companions, flourishing knotted sticks, dance, after their manner, on the top of the instrument.

140. I think we have in this conception as perfect an instance as we require of the lowest supposable phase of immodest or licentious art in music; the "inner consciousness of good" being dim, even in the musician and his audience; and wholly unsympathized with, and unacknowledged, by the Delphian, Vestal, and all other prophetic and cosmic powers. This represented scene came into my mind suddenly, one evening, a few weeks ago, in contrast with another which I was watching in its reality; namely, a group of gentle school-girls, leaning over Mr. Charles Hallè as he was playing a variation on "Home, sweet Home." They had sustained with unwonted courage the glance of subdued indignation with which, having just closed a rippling melody of Sebastian Bach's, (much like what one might fancy the singing of nightingales would be if they fed on honey instead of flies), he turned to the slight, popular air. But they had their own associations with it, and besought for, and obtained it; and pressed close, at first, in vain, to see what no glance could follow, the traversing of the fingers. They soon thought no more of seeing. The wet eyes, round-open, and the little scarlet upper lips, lifted, and drawn slightly together, in passionate glow of utter wonder, became picture-like,—porcelain-like,—in mo-

tionless joy, as the sweet multitude of low notes fell in their timely infinities, like summer rain. Only La Robbia himself (nor even he, unless with tenderer use of colour than is usual in his work) could have rendered some image of that listening.

141. But if the reader can give due vitality in his fancy to these two scenes, he will have in them representative types, clear enough for all future purpose, of the several agencies of debased and perfect art. And the interval may easily and continuously be filled by mediate gradations. Between the entirely immodest, unmeasured, and (in evil sense) unmannered, execution with the fist; and the entirely modest, measured, and (in the noblest sense) mannered, or moral'd, execution with the finger; between the impatient and unpractised doing, containing in itself the witness of lasting impatience and idleness through all previous life, and the patient and practised doing, containing in itself the witness of self-restraint and unwearied toil through all previous life;— between the expressed subject and sentiment of home violation, and the expressed subject and sentiment of home love;—between the sympathy of audience, given in irreverent and contemptuous rage, joyless as the rabidness of a dog, and the sympathy of audience given in an almost appalled humility of intense, rapturous, and yet entirely reasoning and reasonable pleasure;—between these two limits of octave, the reader will find he can class, according to its modesty, usefulness, and grace, or becomingness

all other musical art. For although purity of purpose and fineness of execution by no means go together, degree to degree, (since fine, and indeed all but the finest, work is often spent in the most wanton purpose—as in all our modern opera—and the rudest execution is again often joined with purest purpose, as in a mother's song to her child), still the entire accomplishment of music is only in the union of both. For the difference between that "all but" finest and "finest" is an infinite one; and besides this, however the power of the performer, once attained, may be afterwards misdirected, in slavery to popular passion or childishness, and spend itself, at its sweetest, in idle melodies, cold and ephemeral (like Michael Angelo's snow statue in the other art), or else in vicious difficulty and miserable noise—crackling of thorns under the pot of public sensuality—still, the attainment of this power, and the maintenance of it, involve always in the executant some virtue or courage of high kind; the understanding of which, and of the difference between the discipline which develops it and the disorderly efforts of the amateur, it will be one of our first businesses to estimate rightly. And though not indeed by degree to degree, yet in essential relation (as of winds to waves, the one being always the true cause of the other, though they are not necessarily of equal force at the same time), we shall find vice in its varieties, with art-failure,— and virtue in its varieties, with art-success,—fall and rise together: the peasant-girl's song at her spinning-wheel, the peasant-labourer's "to the oaks and rills,"—domestic music, feebly yet sensitively skilful,—music for the multitude, of beneficent, or of traitorous power,— dance-melodies, pure and orderly, or foul and frantic,— march-music, blatant in mere fever of animal pugnacity, or majestic with force of national duty and memory,—song-music, reckless, sensual, sickly, slovenly, forgetful even of the foolish words it effaces with foolish noise,—or thoughtful, sacred, healthful, artful, for ever sanctifying noble thought with separately distinguished loveliness of belonging sound,—all these families and gradations of good or evil, however mingled, follow, in so far as they are good, one constant law of virtue (or "life-strength," which is the literal meaning of the word, and its intended one, in wise men's mouths), and in so far as they are evil, are evil by outlawry and unvirtue, or death-weakness. Then, passing wholly beyond the domain of death, we may still imagine the ascendant nobleness of the art, through all the concordant life of incorrupt creatures, and a continually deeper harmony of "*puissant* words and murmurs made to bless," until we reach

"The undisturbed song of pure consent,
Aye sung before the sapphire-coloured throne."

142. And so far as the sister arts can be conceived to have place or office, their virtues are subject to a law absolutely the same as that of music, only extending its authority into more various conditions, owing to the introduction of a distinctly representative and historical

power, which acts under logical as well as mathematical restrictions, and is capable of endlessly changeful fault, fallacy, and defeat, as well as of endlessly manifold victory.

143. Next to Modesty, and her delight in measures, let us reflect a little on the character of her adversary, the Goddess of Liberty, and her delight in absence of measures, or in false ones. It is true that there are liberties and liberties. Yonder torrent, crystal-clear, and arrow-swift, with its spray leaping into the air like white troops of fawns, is free enough. Lost, presently, amidst bankless, boundless marsh—soaking in slow shallowness, as it will, hither and thither, listless, among the poisonous reeds and unresisting slime—it is free also. We may choose which liberty we like,—the restraint of voiceful rock, or the dumb and edgeless shore of darkened sand. Of that evil liberty, which men are now glorifying, and proclaiming as essence of gospel to all the earth, and will presently, I suppose, proclaim also to the stars, with invitation to them *out* of their courses,—and of its opposite continence, which is the clasp and χρυσέη περόνη of Aglaia's cestus, we must try to find out something true. For no quality of Art has been more powerful in its influence on public mind; none is more frequently the subject of popular praise, or the end of vulgar effort, than what we call "Freedom." It is necessary to determine the justice or injustice of this popular praise.

144. I said, a little while ago, that the practical teaching of the masters of Art was summed by the O of Giotto.

"You may judge my masterhood of craft," Giotto tells us, "by seeing that I can draw a circle unerringly." And we may safely believe him, understanding him to mean, that—though more may be necessary to an artist than such a power—at least *this* power is necessary. The qualities of hand and eye needful to do this are the first conditions of artistic craft.

145. Try to draw a circle yourself with the "free" hand, and with a single line. You cannot do it if your hand trembles, nor if it hesitates, nor if it is unmanageable, nor if it is in the common sense of the word "free." So far from being free, it must be under a control as absolute and accurate as if it were fastened to an inflexible bar of steel. And yet it must move, under this necessary control, with perfect, untormented serenity of ease.

146. That is the condition of all good work whatsoever. All freedom is error. Every line you lay down is either right or wrong: it may be timidly and awkwardly wrong, or fearlessly and impudently wrong: the aspect of the impudent wrongness is pleasurable to vulgar persons; and is what they commonly call "free" execution: the timid, tottering, hesitating wrongness is rarely so attractive; yet sometimes, if accompanied with good qualities, and right aims in other directions, it becomes in a manner charming, like the inarticulateness of a child: but, whatever the charm or manner of the error, there is but one question ultimately to be asked respecting every line you draw, Is it right or wrong? If right, it most assuredly

is not a " free " line, but an intensely continent, restrained, and considered line ; and the action of the hand in laying it is just as decisive, and just as "free" as the hand of a firstrate surgeon in a critical incision. A great operator told me that his hand could check itself within about the two-hundredth of an inch, in penetrating a membrane; and this, of course, without the help of sight, by sensation only. With help of sight, and in action on a substance which does not quiver nor yield, a fine artist's line is measurable in its proposed direction to considerably less than the thousandth of an inch.

A wide freedom, truly!

147. The conditions of popular art which most foster the common ideas about freedom, are merely results of irregularly energetic effort by men imperfectly educated; these conditions being variously mingled with cruder mannerisms resulting from timidity, or actual imperfection of body. Northern hands and eyes are, of course, never so subtle as Southern; and in very cold countries, artistic execution is palsied. The effort to break through this timidity, or to refine the bluntness, may lead to a licentious impetuosity, or an ostentatious minuteness. Every man's manner has this kind of relation to some defect in his physical powers or modes of thought; so that in the greatest work there is no manner visible. It is at first uninteresting from its quietness; the majesty of restrained power only dawns gradually upon us, as we walk towards its horizon.

There is, indeed, often great delightfulness in the innocent manners of artists who have real power and honesty, and draw, in this way or that, as best they can, under such and such untoward circumstances of life. But the greater part of the looseness, flimsiness, or audacity of modern work is the expression of an inner spirit of licence in mind and heart, connected, as I said, with the peculiar folly of this age, its hope of, and trust in, "liberty." Of which we must reason a little in more general terms.

148. I believe we can nowhere find a better type of a perfectly free creature than in the common house fly. Nor free only, but brave; and irreverent to a degree which I think no human republican could by any philosophy exalt himself to. There is no courtesy in him; he does not care whether it is king or clown whom he teases; and in every step of his swift mechanical march, and in every pause of his resolute observation, there is one and the same expression of perfect egotism, perfect independence and self-confidence, and conviction of the world's having been made for flies. Strike at him with your hand; and to him, the mechanical fact and external aspect of the matter is, what to you it would be, if an acre of red clay, ten feet thick, tore itself up from the ground in one massive field, hovered over you in the air for a second, and came crashing down with an aim. That is the external aspect of it; the inner aspect, to his fly's mind, is of a quite natural and unimportant occurrence—

one of the momentary conditions of his active life. He steps out of the way of your hand, and alights on the back of it. You cannot terrify him, nor govern him, nor persuade him, nor convince him. He has his own positive opinion on all matters; not an unwise one, usually, for his own ends; and will ask no advice of yours. He has no work to do—no tyrannical instinct to obey. The earthworm has his digging; the bee her gathering and building; the spider her cunning net-work; the ant her treasury and accounts. All these are comparatively slaves, or people of vulgar business. But your fly, free in the air, free in the chamber—a black incarnation of caprice— wandering, investigating, flitting, flirting, feasting at his will, with rich variety of choice in feast, from the heaped sweets in the grocer's window to those of the butcher's back-yard, and from the galled place on your cab-horse's back, to the brown spot in the road, from which, as the hoof disturbs him, he rises with angry republican buzz— what freedom is like his?

149. For captivity, again, perhaps your poor watch-dog is as sorrowful a type as you will easily find. Mine certainly is. The day is lovely, but I must write this, and cannot go out with him. He is chained in the yard, because I do not like dogs in rooms, and the gardener does not like dogs in gardens. He has no books,— nothing but his own weary thoughts for company, and a group of those free flies, whom he snaps at, with sullen ill success. Such dim hope as he may have that I may yet

take him out with me, will be, hour by hour, wearily disappointed; or, worse, darkened at once into a leaden despair by an authoritative "No"—too well understood. His fidelity only seals his fate; if he would not watch for me, he would be sent away, and go hunting with some happier master: but he watches, and is wise, and faithful, and miserable: and his high animal intellect only gives him the wistful powers of wonder, and sorrow, and desire, and affection, which embitter his captivity. Yet of the two, would we rather be watch-dog, or fly?

150. Indeed, the first point we have all to determine is not how free we are, but what kind of creatures we are. It is of small importance to any of us whether we get liberty; but of the greatest that we deserve it. Whether we can win it, fate must determine; but that we will be worthy of it, we may ourselves determine; and the sorrowfullest fate, of all that we can suffer, is to have it, *without* deserving it.

151. I have hardly patience to hold my pen and go on writing, as I remember (I would that it were possible for a few consecutive instants to forget) the infinite follies of modern thought in this matter, centred in the notion that liberty is good for a man, irrespectively of the use he is likely to make of it. Folly unfathomable! unspeakable! unendurable to look in the full face of, as the laugh of a cretin. You will send your child, will you, into a room where the table is loaded with sweet wine and fruit—some poisoned, some not?—you will say to him, "Choose

freely, my little child! It is so good for you to have freedom of choice: it forms your character—your individuality! If you take the wrong cup, or the wrong berry, you will die before the day is over, but you will have acquired the dignity of a Free child?"

152. You think that puts the case too sharply? I tell you, lover of liberty, there is no choice offered to you, but it is similarly between life and death. There is no act, nor option of act, possible, but the wrong deed or option has poison in it which will stay in your veins thereafter for ever. Never more to all eternity can you be as you might have been, had you not done that—chosen that. You have "formed your character," forsooth! No; if you have chosen ill, you have De-formed it, and that for ever! In some choices, it had been better for you that a red hot iron bar had struck you aside, scarred and helpless, than that you had so chosen. "You will know better next time!" No. Next time will never come. Next time the choice will be in quite another aspect—between quite different things,—you, weaker than you were by the evil into which you have fallen; it, more doubtful than it was, by the increased dimness of your sight. No one ever gets wiser by doing wrong, nor stronger. You will get wiser and stronger only by doing right, whether forced or not; the prime, the one need is to do *that*, under whatever compulsion, until you can do it without compulsion. And then you are a Man.

153. "What!" a wayward youth might perhaps answer,

incredulously; "no one ever gets wiser by doing wrong? Shall I not know the world best by trying the wrong of it, and repenting? Have I not, even as it is, learned much by many of my errors?" Indeed, the effort by which partially you recovered yourself was precious; that part of your thought by which you discerned the error was precious. What wisdom and strength you kept, and rightly used, are rewarded; and in the pain and the repentance, and in the acquaintance with the aspects of folly and sin, you have learned *something;* how much less than you would have learned in right paths, can never be told, but that it *is* less is certain. Your liberty of choice has simply destroyed for you so much life and strength, never regainable. It is true you now know the habits of swine, and the taste of husks: do you think your father could not have taught you to know better habits and pleasanter tastes, if you had stayed in his house; and that the knowledge you have lost would not have been more, as well as sweeter, than that you have gained? But "it so forms my individuality to be free!" Your individuality was given you by God, and in your race; and if you have any to speak of, you will want no liberty. You will want a den to work in, and peace, and light—no more,—in absolute need; if more, in anywise, it will still not be liberty, but direction, instruction, reproof, and sympathy. But if you have no individuality, if there is no true character nor true desire in you, then you will indeed want to be free. You will begin early; and, as a boy, desire to be a man; and, as a man, think yourself as good as every other. You will choose freely to eat, freely to drink, freely to stagger and fall, freely, at last, to curse yourself and die. Death is the only real freedom possible to us: and that is consummate freedom,—permission for every particle in the rotting body to leave its neighbour particle, and shift for itself. You call it "corruption" in the flesh; but before it comes to that, all liberty is an equal corruption in mind. You ask for freedom of thought; but if you have not sufficient grounds for thought, you have no business to think; and if you have sufficient grounds, you have no business to think wrong. Only one thought is possible to you, if you are wise—your liberty is geometrically proportionate to your folly.

154. "But all this glory and activity of our age; what are they owing to, but to our freedom of thought?" In a measure, they are owing—what good is in them—to the discovery of many lies, and the escape from the power of evil. Not to liberty, but to the deliverance from evil or cruel masters. Brave men have dared to examine lies which had long been taught, not because they were *free-thinkers*, but because they were such stern and close thinkers that the lie could no longer escape them. Of course the restriction of thought, or of its expression, by persecution, is merely a form of violence, justifiable or not, as other violence is, according to the character of the persons against whom it is exercised, and the divine and eter-

nal laws which it vindicates or violates. We must not burn a man alive for saying that the Athanasian creed is ungrammatical, nor stop a bishop's salary because we are getting the worst of an argument with him; neither must we let drunken men howl in the public streets at night. There is much that is true in the part of Mr. Mill's essay on Liberty which treats of freedom of thought; some important truths are there beautifully expressed, but many, quite vital, are omitted; and the balance, therefore, is wrongly struck. The liberty of expression, with a great nation, would become like that in a well-educated company, in which there is indeed freedom of speech, but not of clamour; or like that in an orderly senate, in which men who deserve to be heard, are heard in due time, and under determined restrictions. The degree of liberty you can rightly grant to a number of men is in the inverse ratio of their desire for it; and a general hush, or call to order, would be often very desirable in this England of ours. For the rest, of any good or evil extant, it is impossible to say what measure is owing to restraint, and what to licence where the right is balanced between them. I was not a little provoked one day, a summer or two since, in Scotland, because the Duke of Athol hindered me from examining the gneiss and slate junctions in Glen Tilt, at the hour convenient to me; but I saw them at last, and in quietness; and to the very restriction that annoyed me, owed, probably, the fact of their being in existence, instead of being blasted away by a mob-company; while the "free" paths and inlets of Loch Katrine and the Lake of Geneva are for ever trampled down and destroyed, not by one duke, but by tens of thousands of ignorant tyrants.

155. So, a Dean and Chapter may, perhaps, unjustifiably charge me twopence for seeing a cathedral;—but your free mob pulls spire and all down about my ears, and I can see it no more for ever. And even if I cannot get up to the granite junctions in the glen, the stream comes down from them pure to the Garry ; but in Beddington Park I am stopped by the newly erected fence of a building speculator ; and the bright Wandel, divine of waters as Castaly, is filled by the free public with old shoes, obscene crockery, and ashes.

156. In fine, the arguments for liberty may in general be summed in a few very simple forms, as follows :—

Misguiding is mischievous : therefore guiding is.

If the blind lead the blind, both fall into the ditch : therefore, nobody should lead anybody.

Lambs and fawns should be left free in the fields ; much more bears and wolves.

If a man's gun and shot are his own, he may fire in any direction he pleases.

A fence across a road is inconvenient ; much more one at the side of it.

Babes should not be swaddled with their hands bound down to their sides: therefore they should be thrown out to roll in the kennels naked.

None of these arguments are good, and the practical

issues of them are worse. For there are certain eternal laws for human conduct which are quite clearly discernible by human reason. So far as these are discovered and obeyed, by whatever machinery or authority the obedience is procured, there follow life and strength. So far as they are disobeyed, by whatever good intention the disobedience is brought about, there follow ruin and sorrow. And the first duty of every man in the world is to find his true master, and, for his own good, submit to him; and to find his true inferior, and, for that inferior's good, conquer him. The punishment is sure, if we either refuse the reverence, or are too cowardly and indolent to enforce the compulsion. A base nation crucifies or poisons its wise men, and lets its fools rave and rot in its streets. A wise nation obeys the one, restrains the other, and cherishes all.

157. The best examples of the results of wise normal discipline in Art will be found in whatever evidence remains respecting the lives of great Italian painters, though, unhappily, in eras of progress, but just in proportion to the admirableness and efficiency of the life, will be usually the scantiness of its history. The individualities and liberties which are causes of destruction may be recorded; but the loyal conditions of daily breath are never told. Because Leonardo made models of machines, dug canals, built fortifications, and dissipated half his art-power in capricious ingenuities, we have many anecdotes of him;—but no picture of impor-

tance on canvas, and only a few withered stains of one upon a wall. But because his pupil, or reputed pupil, Luini, laboured in constant and successful simplicity, we have no anecdotes of him;—only hundreds of noble works. Luini is, perhaps, the best central type of the highly-trained Italian painter. He is the only man who entirely united the religious temper which was the spirit-life of art, with the physical power which was its bodily life. He joins the purity and passion of Angelico to the strength of Veronese : the two elements, poised in perfect balance, are so calmed and restrained, each by the other, that most of us lose the sense of both. The artist does not see the strength, by reason of the chastened spirit in which it is used; and the religious visionary does not recognize the passion, by reason of the frank human truth with which it is rendered. He is a man ten times greater than Leonardo;—a mighty colourist, while Leonardo was only a fine draughtsman in black, staining the chiaroscuro drawing, like a coloured print: he perceived and rendered the delicatest types of human beauty that have been painted since the days of the Greeks, while Leonardo depraved his finer instincts by caricature, and remained to the end of his days the slave of an archaic smile: and he is a designer as frank, instinctive, and exhaustless as Tintoret, while Leonardo's design is only an agony of science, admired chiefly because it is painful, and capable of analysis in its best accomplishment. Luini has left nothing behind him that is not lovely; but of his life I believe hardly anything is known beyond remnants of tradition which murmur about Lugano and Saronno, and which remain ungleaned. This only is certain, that he was born in the loveliest district of North Italy, where hills, and streams, and air, meet in softest harmonies. Child of the Alps, and of their divinest lake, he is taught, without doubt or dismay, a lofty religious creed, and a sufficient law of life, and of its mechanical arts. Whether lessoned by Leonardo himself, or merely one of many, disciplined in the system of the Milanese school, he learns unerringly to draw, unerringly and enduringly to paint. His tasks are set him without question day by day, by men who are justly satisfied with his work, and who accept it without any harmful praise, or senseless blame. Place, scale, and subject are determined for him on the cloister wall or the church dome; as he is required, and for sufficient daily bread, and little more, he paints what he has been taught to design wisely, and has passion to realize gloriously: every touch he lays is eternal, every thought he conceives is beautiful and pure: his hand moves always in radiance of blessing; from day to day his life enlarges in power and peace; it passes away cloudlessly, the starry twilight remaining arched far against the night.

158. Oppose to such a life as this that of a great painter amidst the elements of modern English liberty. Take the life of Turner, in whom the artistic energy and inherent love of beauty were at least as strong as in

Luini: but, amidst the disorder and ghastliness of the lower streets of London, his instincts in early infancy were warped into toleration of evil, or even into delight in it. He gathers what he can of instruction by questioning and prying among half-informed masters; spells out some knowledge of classical fable; educates himself, by an admirable force, to the production of wildly majestic or pathetically tender and pure pictures, by which he cannot live. There is no one to judge them, or to command him: only some of the English upper classes hire him to paint their houses and parks, and destroy the drawings afterwards by the most wanton neglect. Tired of labouring carefully, without either reward or praise, he dashes out into various experimental and popular works—makes himself the servant of the lower public, and is dragged hither and thither at their will; while yet, helpless and guideless, he indulges his idiosyncrasies till they change into insanities; the strength of his soul increasing its sufferings, and giving force to its errors; all the purpose of life degenerating into instinct; and the web of his work wrought, at last, of beauties too subtle to be understood, his liberty, with vices too singular to be forgiven—all useless, because magnificent idiosyncrasy had become solitude, or contention, in the midst of a reckless populace, instead of submitting itself in loyal harmony to the Art-laws of an understanding nation. And the life passed away in darkness; and its final work, in all the best beauty of it, has already perished, only enough remaining to teach us what we have lost.

159. These are the opposite effects of Law and of Liberty on men of the highest powers. In the case of inferiors the contrast is still more fatal : under strict law, they become the subordinate workers in great schools, healthily aiding, echoing, or supplying, with multitudinous force of hand, the mind of the leading masters : they are the nameless carvers of great architecture—stainers of glass—hammerers of iron—helpful scholars, whose work ranks round, if not with, their master's, and never disgraces it. But the inferiors under a system of licence for the most part perish in miserable effort;* a few struggle into pernicious emi-

---

* As I correct this sheet for press, my *Pall Mall Gazette* of last Saturday, April 17th, is lying on the table by me. I print a few lines out of it :—

"An Artist's Death.—A sad story was told at an inquest held in St. Pancras last night by Dr. Lankester on the body of * * *, aged fifty-nine, a French artist, who was found dead in his bed at his rooms in * * * Street. M. * * *, also an artist, said he had known the deceased for fifteen years. He once held a high position, and being anxious to make a name in the world, he five years ago commenced a large picture, which he hoped, when completed, to have in the gallery at Versailles ; and with that view he sent a photograph of it to the French Emperor. He also had an idea of sending it to the English Royal Academy. He laboured on this picture, neglecting other work which would have paid him well, and gradually sank lower and lower into poverty. His friends assisted him, but being absorbed in his great work, he did not heed their advice, and they left him. He was, however, assisted by the French Ambassador, and last Saturday he (the witness) saw de-

nence—harmful alike to themselves and to all who admire them; many die of starvation; many insane, either in weakness of insolent egotism, like Haydon, or in a conscientious agony of beautiful purpose and warped power, like Blake. There is no probability of the persistence of a licentious school in any good accidentally discovered by them; there is an approximate certainty of their gathering, with acclaim, round any shadow of evil, and following *it* to whatever quarter of destruction it may lead.

160. Thus far the notes on Freedom. Now, lastly, here is some talk which I tried at the time to make intelligible; and with which I close this volume, because it will serve sufficiently to express the practical relation in which I think the art and imagination of the Greeks stand to our own; and will show the reader that my view of that relation is unchanged, from the first day on which I began to write, until now.

ceased, who was much depressed in spirits, as he expected the brokers to be put in possession for rent. He said his troubles were so great that he feared his brain would give way. The witness gave him a shilling, for which he appeared very thankful. On Monday the witness called upon him, but received no answer to his knock. He went again on Tuesday, and entered the deceased's bedroom and found him dead. Dr. George Ross said that when called in to the deceased he had been dead at least two days. The room was in a filthy dirty condition, and the picture referred to—certainly a very fine one—was in that room. The post-mortem examination shewed that the cause of death was fatty degeneration of the heart, the latter probably having ceased its action through the mental excitement of the deceased."

THE HERCULES OF CAMARINA.

Address to the Students of the Art School of South Lambeth, March 15th, 1869.

161. AMONG the photographs of Greek coins which present so many admirable subjects for your study, I must speak for the present of one only: the Hercules of Camarina. You have, represented by a Greek workman, in that coin, the face of a man, and the skin of a lion's head. And the man's face is like a man's face, but the lion's skin is not like a lion's skin.

162. Now there are some people who will tell you that Greek art is fine, because it is true; and because it carves men's faces as like men's faces as it can.

And there are other people who will tell you that Greek art is fine because it is not true; and carves a lion's skin so as to look not at all like a lion's skin.

And you fancy that one or other of these sets of people must be wrong, and are perhaps much puzzled to find out which you should believe.

But neither of them are wrong, and you will have eventually to believe, or rather to understand and know, in reconciliation, the truths taught by each;—but for the present, the teachers of the first group are those you must follow.

It is they who tell you the deepest and usefullest truth, which involves all others in time. *Greek art, and all other art, is fine when it makes a man's face as like a man's face as it can.* Hold to that. All kinds of nonsense are talked to you, now-a-days, ingeniously and irrelevantly about art. Therefore, for the most part of the day, shut your ears, and keep your eyes open: and understand primarily, what you may, I fancy, understand easily, that the greatest masters of all greatest schools—Phidias, Donatello, Titian, Velasquez, or Sir Joshua Reynolds—all tried to make human creatures as like human creatures as they could ; and that anything less like humanity than their work, is not so good as theirs.

Get that well driven into your heads; and don't let it out again, at your peril.

163. Having got it well in, you may then farther understand, safely, that there is a great deal of secondary work in pots, and pans, and floors, and carpets, and shawls, and architectural ornament, which ought, essentially, to be *unlike* reality, and to depend for its charm on quite other qualities than imitative ones. But all such art is inferior and secondary—much of it more or less instinctive and animal, and a civilized human creature can only learn its principles rightly, by knowing those of great civilized art first—which is always the representation, to the utmost of its power of whatever it has got to show—made to look as like the thing as possible. Go into the National Gallery, and look at the foot of Correggio's Venus there. Correggio made it as like a foot as he could, and you won't easily find anything liker. Now, you will find on any Greek vase something meant for a foot, or a hand, which is not at all like one. The Greek

vase is a good thing in its way, but Correggio's picture is the best work.

164. So, again, go into the Turner room of the National Gallery, and look at Turner's drawing of "Ivy Bridge." You will find the water in it is like real water, and the ducks in it are like real ducks. Then go into the British Museum, and look for an Egyptian landscape, and you will find the water in that constituted of blue zigzags, not at all like water; and ducks in the middle of it made of red lines, looking not in the least as if they could stand stuffing with sage and onions. They are very good in their way, but Turner's are better.

165. I will not pause to fence my general principle against what you perfectly well know of the due contradiction,—that a thing may be painted very like, yet painted ill. Rest content with knowing that it *must* be like, if it is painted well; and take this farther general law:—Imitation is like charity. When it is done for love it is lovely; when it is done for show, hateful.

166. Well, then, this Greek coin is fine, first, because the face is like a face. Perhaps you think there is something particularly handsome in the face, which you can't see in the photograph, or can't at present appreciate. But there is nothing of the kind. It is a very regular, quiet, commonplace sort of face; and any average English gentleman's, of good descent, would be far handsomer.

167. Fix that in your heads also, therefore, that Greek

faces are not particularly beautiful. Of the much nonsense against which you are to keep your ears shut, that which is talked to you of the Greek ideal of beauty, is among the absolutest. There is not a single instance of a very beautiful head left by the highest school of Greek art. On coins, there is even no approximately beautiful one. The Juno of Argos is a virago; the Athena of Athens grotesque; the Athena of Corinth is insipid; and of Thurium, sensual. The Siren Ligeia, and fountain of Arethusa, on the coins of Terina and Syracuse, are prettier, but totally without expression, and chiefly set off by their well-curled hair. You might have expected something subtle in Mercuries; but the Mercury of Ænus is a very stupid-looking fellow, in a cap like a bowl, with a knob on the top of it. The Bacchus of Thasos is a drayman with his hair pomatum'd. The Jupiter of Syracuse is, however, calm and refined; and the Apollo of Clazomenæ would have been impressive, if he had not come down to us much flattened by friction. But on the whole, the merit of Greek coins does not primarily depend on beauty of features, nor even, in the period of highest art, that of the statues. You may take the Venus of Melos as a standard of beauty of the central Greek type. She has tranquil, regular, and lofty features; but could not hold her own for a moment against the beauty of a simple English girl, of pure race and kind heart.

168. And the reason that Greek art, on the whole, bores you, (and you know it does,) is that you are always

forced to look in it for something that is not there; but which may be seen every day, in real life, all round you; and which you are naturally disposed to delight in, and ought to delight in. For the Greek race was not at all one of exalted beauty, but only of general and healthy completeness of form. They were only, and could be only, beautiful in body to the degree that they were beautiful in soul; (for you will find, when you read deeply into the matter, that the body is only the soul made visible). And the Greeks were indeed very good people, much better people than most of us think, or than many of us are; but there are better people alive now than the best of them, and lovelier people to be seen now, than the loveliest of them.

169. Then, what *are* the merits of this Greek art, which make it so exemplary for you? Well, not that it is beautiful, but that it is Right.* All that it desires to do, it does, and all that it does, does well. You will find, as you advance in the knowledge of art, that its laws of self-restraint are very marvellous; that its peace of heart, and contentment in doing a simple thing, with only one or two qualities, restrictedly desired, and sufficiently attained, are a most wholesome element of education for you, as opposed to the wild writhing, and wrestling, and longing for the moon, and tilting at windmills, and agony of eyes, and torturing of fingers, and general spinning out of one's soul into fiddlestrings, which constitute the ideal life of a modern artist.

* Compare above, § 101.

Also observe, there is entire masterhood of its business up to the required point. A Greek does not reach after other people's strength, nor out-reach his own. He never tries to paint before he can draw; he never tries to lay on flesh where there are no bones; and he never expects to find the bones of anything in his inner consciousness. Those are his first merits—sincere and innocent purpose, strong common sense and principle, and all the strength that comes of these, and all the grace that follows on that strength.

170. But, secondly, Greek art is always exemplary in disposition of masses, which is a thing that in modern days students rarely look for, artists not enough, and the public never. But, whatever else Greek work may fail of, you may be always sure its masses are well placed, and their placing has been the object of the most subtle care. Look, for instance, at the inscription in front of this Hercules of the name of the town—Camarina. You can't read it, even though you may know Greek, without some pains; for the sculptor knew well enough that it mattered very little whether you read it or not, for the Camarina Hercules could tell his own story; but what did above all things matter was, that no K or A or M should come in a wrong place with respect to the outline of the head, and divert the eye from it, or spoil any of its lines. So the whole inscription is thrown into a sweeping curve of gradually diminishing size, continuing from the lion's paws, round the neck, up to the forehead, and answering a decorative purpose as completely as the curls of the mane opposite.

Of these, again, you cannot change or displace one without mischief: they are almost as even in reticulation as a piece of basket-work; but each has a different form and a due relation to the rest, and if you set to work to draw that mane rightly, you will find that, whatever time you give to it, you can't get the tresses quite into their places, and that every tress out of its place does an injury. If you want to test your powers of accurate drawing, you may make that lion's mane your *pons asinorum*. I have never yet met with a student who didn't make an ass in a lion's skin of himself, when he tried it.

171. Granted, however, that these tresses may be finely placed, still they are not like a lion's mane. So we come back to the question,—if the face is to be like a man's face, why is not the lion's mane to be like a lion's mane? Well, because it can't be like a lion's mane without too much trouble;—and inconvenience after that, and poor success, after all. Too much trouble, in cutting the die into fine fringes and jags; inconvenience after that,—because fringes and jags would spoil the surface of a coin; poor success after all,—because, though you can easily stamp cheeks and foreheads smooth at a blow, you can't stamp projecting tresses fine at a blow, whatever pains you take with your die.

So your Greek uses his common sense, wastes no time, loses no skill, and says to you, "Here are beautifully set tresses, which I have carefully designed and easily stamped. Enjoy them; and if you cannot understand that they mean lion's mane, heaven mend your wits."

172. See then, you have in this work, well-founded knowledge, simple and right aims, thorough mastery of handicraft, splendid invention in arrangement, unerring common sense in treatment,—merits, these, I think, exemplary enough to justify our tormenting you a little with Greek Art. But it has one merit more than these, the greatest of all. It always means something worth saying. Not merely worth saying for that time only, but for all time. What do you think this helmet of lion's hide is always given to Hercules for? You can't suppose it means only that he once killed a lion, and always carried its skin afterwards to show that he had, as Indian sportsmen send home stuffed rugs, with claws at the corners, and a lump in the middle which one tumbles over every time one stirs the fire. What *was* this Nemean Lion, whose spoils were evermore to cover Hercules from the cold? Not merely a large specimen of Felis Leo, ranging the fields of Nemea, be sure of that. This Nemean cub was one of a bad litter. Born of Typhon and Echidna,—of the whirlwind and the snake,—Cerberus his brother, the Hydra of Lerna his sister,—it must have been difficult to get his hide off him. He had to be found in darkness too, and dealt upon without weapons, by grip at the throat—arrows and club of no avail against him. What does all that mean?

173. It means that the Nemean Lion is the first great adversary of life, whatever that may be—to Hercules, or

to any of us, then or now. The first monster we have to strangle, or be destroyed by, fighting in the dark, and with none to help us, only Athena standing by, to encourage with her smile. Every man's Nemean Lion lies in wait for him somewhere. The slothful man says, there is a lion in the path. He says well. The quiet *un*slothful man says the same, and knows it too. But they differ in their farther reading of the text. The slothful man says I shall be slain, and the unslothful, rr shall be. It is the first ugly and strong enemy that rises against us, all future victory depending on victory over that. Kill it; and through all the rest of life, what was once dreadful is your armour and you are clothed with that conquest for every other, and helmed with its crest of fortitude for evermore.

Alas, we have most of us to walk bare-headed; but that is the meaning of the story of Nemea,—worth laying to heart and thinking of, sometimes, when you see a dish garnished with parsley, which was the crown at the Nemean games.

174. How far, then, have we got, in our list of the merits of Greek art now?

Sound knowledge.

Simple aims.

Mastered craft.

Vivid invention.

Strong common sense.

And eternally true and wise meaning.

Are these not enough? Here is one more then, which

will find favour, I should think, with the British Lion. Greek art is never frightened at anything, it is always cool.

175. It differs essentially from all other art, past or present, in this incapability of being frightened. Half the power and imagination of every other school depend on a certain feverish terror mingling with their sense of beauty;—the feeling that a child has in a dark room, or a sick person in seeing ugly dreams. But the Greeks never have ugly dreams. They cannot draw anything ugly when they try. Sometimes they put themselves to their wits'-end to draw an ugly thing,—the Medusa's head, for instance,—but they can't do it,—not they,—because nothing frightens them. They widen the mouth, and grind the teeth, and puff the cheeks, and set the eyes a-goggling; and the thing is only ridiculous after all, not the least dreadful, for there is no dread in their hearts. Pensiveness; amazement; often deepest grief and desolateness. All these; but terror never. Everlasting calm in the presence of all fate; and joy such as they could win, not indeed in a perfect beauty, but in beauty at perfect rest! A kind of art this, surely, to be looked at, and thought upon sometimes with profit, even in these latter days.

176. To be looked at sometimes. Not continually, and never as a model for imitation. For you are not Greeks; but, for better or worse, English creatures; and cannot do, even if it were a thousand times better worth

doing, anything well, except what your English hearts shall prompt, and your English skies teach you. For all good art is the natural utterance of its own people in its own day.

But also, your own art is a better and brighter one than ever this Greek art was. Many motives, powers, and insights have been added to those elder ones. The very corruptions into which we have fallen are signs of a subtle life, higher than theirs was, and therefore more fearful in its faults and death. Christianity has neither superseded, nor, by itself, excelled heathenism; but it has added its own good, won also by many a Nemean contest in dark valleys, to all that was good and noble in heathenism: and our present thoughts and work, when they are right, are nobler than the heathen's. And we are not reverent enough to them, because we possess too much of them. That sketch of four cherub heads from an English girl, by Sir Joshua Reynolds, at Kensington, is an incomparably finer thing than ever the Greeks did. Ineffably tender in the touch, yet Herculean in power; innocent, yet exalted in feeling; pure in colour as a pearl; reserved and decisive in design, as this Lion crest,—if *it* alone existed of such,— if it were a picture by Zeuxis, the only one left in the world, and you built a shrine for it, and were allowed to see it only seven days in a year, it alone would teach you all of art that you ever needed to know. But you do not learn from this or any other such work, because you have not reverence enough for them, and are trying to learn from all at once, and from a hundred other masters besides.

177. Here, then, is the practical advice which I would venture to deduce from what I have tried to show you. Use Greek art as a first, not a final, teacher. Learn to draw carefully from Greek work; above all, to place forms correctly, and to use light and shade tenderly. Never allow yourselves black shadows. It is easy to make things look round and projecting; but the things to exercise yourselves in are the placing of the masses, and the modelling of the lights. It is an admirable exercise to take a pale wash of colour for all the shadows, never reinforcing it everywhere, but drawing the statue as if it were in far distance, making all the darks one flat pale tint. Then model from those into the lights, rounding as well as you can, on those subtle conditions. In your chalk drawings, separate the lights from the darks at once all over; then reinforce the darks slightly where absolutely necessary, and put your whole strength on the lights and their limits. Then, when you have learned to draw thoroughly, take one master for your painting, as you would have done necessarily in old times by being put into his school (were I to choose for you, it should be among six men only—Titian, Correggio, Paul Veronese, Velasquez, Reynolds, or Holbein). If you are a landscapist, Turner must be your only guide, (for no other great landscape painter has yet lived); and having chosen, do your best to understand your own chosen

master, and obey *him*, and no one else, till you have strength to deal with the nature itself round you, and then, be your own master, and see with your own eyes. If you have got masterhood or sight in you, that is the way to make the most of them; and if you have neither, you will at least be sound in your work, prevented from immodest and useless effort, and protected from vulgar and fantastic error.

And so I wish you all, good speed, and the favour of Hercules and of the Muses; and to those who shall best deserve them, the crown of Parsley first, and then of the Laurel.

THE END.

www.ingramcontent.com/pod-product-compliance
Lightning Source LLC
Chambersburg PA
CBHW031441160426
43195CB00010BB/807